How Parents Can Help Kids Improve Test Scores

Taking the Stakes Out of Literacy Testing

2nd Edition

Steven Schneider

ROWMAN & LITTLEFIELD EDUCATION

A division of
ROWMAN & LITTLEFIELD
Lanham • Boulder • New York • Toronto • Plymouth, UK

Published by Rowman & Littlefield Education
A division of Rowman & Littlefield
4501 Forbes Boulevard, Suite 200, Lanham, Maryland 20706
www.rowman.com

10 Thornbury Road, Plymouth PL6 7PP, United Kingdom

British Library Cataloguing in Publication Information Available

Library of Congress Cataloging-in-Publication Data

Schneider, Steven, 1947–
   How parents can help kids improve test scores : taking the stakes out of literacy testing / Steven Schneider. — Second edition.
      pages cm
   Includes bibliographical references and index.
   ISBN 978-1-61048-959-1 (cloth : alk. paper) — ISBN 978-1-61048-960-7 (pbk. : alk. paper) — ISBN 978-1-61048-961-4 (electronic) 1. Reading—Ability testing. 2. Test-taking skills—Study and teaching. 3. Education—Parent participation. I. Title.
   LB1050.46.S36 2014
   372.48'4—dc23   2013034523

∞™ The paper used in this publication meets the minimum requirements of American National Standard for Information Sciences—Permanence of Paper for Printed Library Materials, ANSI/NISO Z39.48-1992.

Printed in the United States of America

This book is dedicated to
Sherry, Erica, Jeremy, and Tracey
who brighten my life with both their
joy of learning and their joy of living.

Contents

Preface   vii

Introduction: The Road to Literacy   xiii

1 What Are Standardized Tests?   1

2 Understanding the New Standards   7

3 Parents Can Make the Difference   11

4 What to Expect Students Will Encounter on a Standardized Test   15

5 Taking Another Look   23

6 The Flip Side of Testing   29

7 A Quiet Place   31

8 Pinpoint Reading Overview: Review—Read—Reinforce—Retell   35

9 The Art of Questioning   49

10 Pairing and Sharing   57

11 Note Taking   61

12 Probing   65

13 Phonics   71

14 The Strategic Reader   75

15 Writing 81

16 Writing with the New Common Core Standards in Mind 91

17 Keeping It Positive 95

18 The Night Before 97

19 Getting the Results 99

20 A Pinpoint Reading Bibliography 105

21 Using EBooks 109

22 Making Literature Come Alive 111

23 A Troubleshooting Guide 121

24 Toolbox: The Top Twelve Skills 135

25 Useful Websites 149

26 Final Thoughts 151

Appendix A: Graphic Organizers, Templates, Forms 155

Appendix B: Sample Story with Lesson Plan 163

References 175

Preface

BUILDING BRIDGES TO
LITERACY—PARENTS, TEACHERS, KIDS

Since the first edition of *How Parents Can Help Kids Improve Test Scores* was published in 2006, reading instruction hasn't really changed that much. Yes, we now have newly improvised and mandated state standards and tests geared to those standards. And we also have a plethora of choices of reading thanks in part to the burgeoning of the ebook markets and more sophisticated computer materials. Teachers may be better trained, those that, indeed, actually receive an adequate amount of staff development.

Still the onus is squarely on the teacher and parent to serve as a beacon and a driving force moving our children down that long road to literacy in reading and writing. Never before have teachers been held accountable for reading progress and achievement on standardized reading tests. Parents feel the pressure, too; making sure their kids are getting the right type of literacy education to help them, among other things, prepare for their state's standardized testing.

Much has been said about most states adopting the Common Core State Standards. Yet it doesn't guarantee that following these standards contributes toward success later in life. It will be many years before parents know the true effect of these new standards and how they influence testing. Yet high stakes testing still exists nationwide. Being able to read and understand the printed word has a profound effect on how our children make progress in their lives. How well they do in school, what type of job they get, and how they become a functional contributing member of our society depend on them being literate.

Being competent in reading and writing can serve to open doors for our children that might forever be locked in their search to find their own worth, potential, and capabilities. This book can serve both parents and teachers to help children reach their full potential, enrich their lives through fostering the love of literature as well as demonstrate success on standardized reading tests. The key to success is becoming a life-long literate person in and out of school.

Literacy involves learning reading, writing, listening, and speaking skills. It is the ability to use these skills to learn the subject matter and the content of anything that is written or spoken. It describes how skillful and knowledgeable a person can be. It suggests a child's ability to read and write a language.

In short, educators and parents can play a pivotal role in helping children develop the literacy skills that are needed to construct knowledge, discover new concepts and ideas, and clarify and obtain meaning from the printed word. Literacy is the ability one must have to fully function and contribute effectively and positively in a society that underscores the importance of reading. The act of learning to read takes great effort and hard work. It involves standards and objectives as well as the standardized tests used to measure whether those standards are being met.

But what really mattered and where the strength really lay was with teacher competency, enthusiasm, and attitude. The vehicle for success also involved another factor that was an integral part of the success equation: watchful parents who carefully monitored their child's progress.

This surveillance increased proportionally with the level of a teacher's capabilities. Weak teachers evoked more parental involvement; strong teachers, less. Sometimes the opposite was true. Nevertheless, teachers and parents have a joint responsibility to create a nurturing educational environment that is both loving and supportive.

It's hard to say exactly what variables affect education the most, but it's safe to say that if a parent gives some form of direct assistance in conjunction with the homeroom teacher's instruction on a daily basis, positive things can occur. Help is needed for those students who are doing well but especially for those who simply need more help than the school can give. My father used to say that trying things might not help—but it couldn't hurt.

It is possible and probable that any one school-based reading program can actually guarantee success. Educators still advocate and rightly so, that appropriate, genuine parental intervention on a daily basis can only serve to better a child's education and will probably lead to the eventual achievement of a higher degree of literacy. Scoring high on reading tests is but one measure of that kind of achievement, and teachers and parents alike want to see children score higher. You want them to go for the gold. You want them to grab the ring off the merry-go-round and not merely pass it by.

This book can help you do just that by following a program called Pinpoint Reading. Pinpoint Reading is designed to

- ensure academic success by giving educators the tools necessary to improve their students' reading skills and in turn increase students' scores on standardized reading tests given in schools.
- sustain and support current literacy programs offered by schools by giving extra support as teachers and parents enhance the literacy skills of reading, writing, listening, and speaking.
- provide support by offering strategies and activities to directly improve decoding (the act of transforming written words into spoken words) using phonics knowledge; increase vocabulary knowledge and reading comprehension skills, which are critical in order to derive meaning from text; and improve fluency, which will help children to be able to read orally with speed, accuracy, and proper expression.
- develop specific strategies that will help improve test-taking skills and prepare students to become more cognizant of the structure and purpose of standardized reading tests given in school systems throughout the United States, which will in turn help students increase their scores.
- build and sustain a child's self-esteem, confidence, and motivation, as these factors nurture a positive attitude toward reading books, and assist parents in developing a motivational and exciting home reading support program.
- enhance writing skills by preparing students to properly address the expectations of the writing portions embedded within standardized reading tests.
- foster an appreciation of literature and a respect for reading and learning by sharing the fun and enjoyment of reading.

In study after study, parents can, and do, make a difference in their child's overall achievement. Parents will have to do more than just superficially check to see that homework is done nightly. The link between parental involvement and a student's performance is critical, and its potential value is limitless.

It has been shown that when parents participated in at-school and at-home activities, their children made significant gains in language scores as compared to those whose parents were less involved. Current research finds that parental involvement has a positive impact on student achievement. This outcome holds across families of all economic, racial, and ethnic backgrounds and for children of all ages. Specifically, when parents are involved in schools to support learning, students perform better on tests and earn higher grades:

> The evidence is consistent, positive, and convincing. Families have a major influence on their children's achievement in school. When schools and families work together to support learning, children tend to do better in school, stay in school longer, and like school more. (Mapp, 2003)

In another study, Shaver and Walls (1998) found that children whose parents were given workshops on how to help their children at home had increased gains in reading and math skills, as measured by standardized tests, when compared with children whose parents did not attend or had uneven attendance.

Moreover, a study done by several researchers concluded that parental involvement correlates with academic success. The study examined student achievement in reading and math, as well as attendance. One of the measures involved a questionnaire gauging the extent of parents' educational activities at home. The findings again supported what we know is true: when parents were involved at home and at school, student academic performance was good. The researchers found that engagement in home learning activities was the strongest positive predictor for math and reading achievement (Izzo et al., 1999).

Even families of non-English-speaking students can participate. Parents of non-English-speaking students can seek help implementing a support program by consulting with teachers and specialists at their child's school. Parents may want to seek remedial help to improve their own skills before attempting a home program; this assistance will serve to boost their confidence about how to more effectively help their children.

For instance, parents can take workshops at school or attend adult education classes. Schools can help by holding bilingual programs for parents who need to advance their language skills and facility in English.

Strong home literacy support is a no-brainer. Parents who, with the support of their child's teachers, are involved in their child's work often improve their child's school performance. Some educators say that a parent cannot be expected to teach the actual skills of reading to their children, that teaching the skills of reading is a highly complex process that requires planning and effort by highly trained professionals.

Yet, parents can support a teacher's efforts. They can help to improve what has already been taught. A parent can also help a child establish a positive attitude toward reading. Today, we bear witness to students gravitating toward electronic media to satisfy and fulfill their interests to the exclusion of sound educational activities. Seldom do we see children with books in hand. They are becoming increasingly dependent on video games, television, and computers.

Our obligation is to show children that reading is an important and necessary part of everyday life. People must be able to read and write in order to become fully functional and capable literate citizens who possess the will and the ability to make important contributions to our society. Therefore, maintaining and fostering the bonds between teacher, parent, and child is critical.

The first step is to find out what areas a child needs improvement in. Teachers, parents, administrators, and school specialists must communicate any concerns to one another before the first report card comes home. Parents should find out about the testing schedule before school starts and plan strategies. As a family, they can talk together and plan how everyone can help out. If parents can't help out one evening, then maybe an older sibling can step in to fill the void.

Parents can complete the Parent Reading Interest Survey in Figure 1.1 (p. 2) to help plan a home reading program.

Children learn to read by reading every day. The more they read, the more they will better understand what they are reading, and the better readers they will become.

Introduction: The Road to Literacy

Parents need to become familiar with what it is that teachers, principals, and school systems want from their children. Do you know what your state's proposed standards in reading, writing, and other aspects of literacy are? After discussing the standards which you need to know to help your child succeed on standardized tests in literacy, we explore the ways teachers and parents can communicate their mutual needs, goals, and objectives.

This second edition reveals the need for parents and teachers to become thoroughly familiar with what standardized tests are and what teachers and parents should expect their children will encounter. With this knowledge of your state's testing format, parents will be ready to give direct, specific instructions with their children augmenting their teacher and school district's plan, by following the step-by-step author-developed process outlined on these pages referred to as "Pinpoint Reading," which is a reading at home process to help their child become a better strategic reader.

After the process is clarified, parents and teachers can learn about the specific types of comprehension questions to ask, the process of coordinating what parents can do with what is actually happening in the classroom as well as teaching children about the importance of note-taking, probing to find specific material in reading passages, and by using phonics strategies.

The chapter on strategic reading emphasizes metacognitive skills that can help your child increase their comprehension skills. The section on writing emphasizes the learning of specific writing skills and strategies and what types of writing skills are required on standardized tests as children learn to write in different styles and genres in response to what they are reading.

The program outlined here can help parents learn about general and specific test preparation skills as they pertain to developing an educationally nurturing home environment.

Emphasis on using good quality books obtained through library, ebooks, and assorted bibliography information is revealed as well as a troubleshooting guide and a toolbox in order to strengthen literary skills at home. Useful hands-on parent-child activities that even teachers can use to enhance learning and literacy is discussed. Parents and teachers can get up to date, timely, and relevant practical information on all aspects of test preparation.

This book also offers a short story-memoir that both teachers and parents can use. It is accompanied by a sample lesson plan that can be utilized at home or at school.

This book emphasizes how parents can more directly take charge in helping their child achieve better results on standardized reading achievement tests. It also serves to build bridges between school officials and teachers, which are extremely critical as we guide our children down the path to literacy so they may realize success in life.

Chapter One

What Are Standardized Tests?

No matter what school they are attending, students are required to take standardized tests in reading and language arts, math, science, social studies, and writing. Standardized tests have always been around. They will not disappear. Schools across the country have turned to standardized tests to evaluate and assess their students' performance.

Individual states are responsible for measuring every public school's student progress in reading and math in grades 3 through 8 and at least once during the 10th through 12th grades. Schools are obligated to show adequate yearly progress to their states. Federal government regulations stipulate that students will have to show proficiency in reading, writing, math, and other disciplines.

Standardized tests are used to determine a child's strengths and weaknesses, but some researchers have concluded that these types of tests generally have questionable ability to predict a child's academic success. They should not be used as the exclusive predictor of a student's ability and achievement. Yet within American schools, standardized testing has become the sole evaluation of a child's overall performance, ability, and future achievement levels.

A standardized test, or any test for that matter, is simply a measure of one's ability on any given day and should not be used as the only tool to measure literacy growth. But all too often the reality is that it is.

Standardized testing and annual school report cards help teachers determine their students' strengths and weaknesses. With this information, teachers are able to plan lessons according to standards that need to be met and concentrate on the student's present and future needs.

	Always	Seldom	Never
1. I often read at home and model this behavior.			
2. I allow my child to watch television as much as he or she wants.			
3. My child has an ample supply of books.			
4. I take my child to the library.			
5. I buy books for presents.			
6. I encourage my child to read in the car.			
7. I read aloud to my child.			
8. I help my child with his or her reading homework.			
9. I help my child prepare for reading tests.			
10. I provide a quiet area for my child's studies.			
11. I provide a variety of athletic, cultural, and social activities for my child.			
12. I carefully monitor my child's progress at school.			
13. I take an interest in my child's schoolwork.			
14. I encourage my child to use his or her spare time wisely by reading and then discussing what he or she read.			
15. I discuss what books my child is reading at the dinner table.			
16. I talk about school and what my child is currently reading and why.			
17. I play popular word games like Scrabble, crossword puzzles, word jumbles, or word-finds found in newspapers and magazines.			
18. My child participates in school book clubs.			
19. My child subscribes to one of his or her favorite magazines.			

Figure 1.1. Parent Reading Interest Survey

However, standardized tests pose a variety of problems within the classroom. Teachers are so preoccupied trying to cram material into the curriculum that they wind up teaching to and for the test. They are practically unable to provide an exciting, different, and creative learning environment, at least until the test is over. Teaching toward a test does nothing to differentiate learners, their intelligences, and their abilities.

Standardized testing is used as a practical tool to gain funding from state and federal sources for school districts, assess a student's performance, and predict a student's future performance. The problem with an overemphasis on standardized testing is that it gives the teacher an unofficial mandate to "teach to the test," specifically avoiding deep critical analysis, creative thinking, and individual differences and needs.

Teachers merely become coaches or glorified tutors of test-taking skills. Standardized testing can lead to a lack of sensitivity to a particular child's social issues and concerns. Moreover, students are being instructed to learn one set approach for a particular exam that is formatted for mass distribution. This can only be perceived as detrimental to a child's self-esteem as it can debilitate a student's perspective of what a meaningful education should be.

Standardized tests generally have questionable ability to predict one's academic success. However, it can be noted that some if not all of the test-taking strategies may, at least in the short term, help children with organization and interpretation of reading matter as well as improving note-taking and writing skills.

Within American schools, standardized testing has become the sole evaluation of a child's overall performance and ability, and the only predictor of future achievement. In most cases, standardized tests are the brunt of a continuous debate as to their effectiveness, usefulness, validity, and reliability. Since standardized tests are mass produced and relatively inexpensive to administer, with usually one teacher for an entire class, they can be managed and mandated simply and deliver visible results in a few months.

It is for this reason that municipalities, including our federal government, have come to view standardized testing as the only reliable means for performance-based accountability. Instead of accurately assessing performance, test items are deliberately selected to maximize the difference between high-level questions and low-level questions and are therefore used to shunt children into different classes, programs, and schools.

Since test makers seem to ignore a child's experiences in life, cultural and language variations, and variations in the quality of educational experiences, tests of this nature fall short of accurately measuring a child's performance. Standardized tests have been proven to contain flaws and biases that create a multitude of gaps in their performance. Children think differently. They operate on several intelligence levels, some of which may not be revealed by standardized testing.

In the end, creative thinking and critical thinking take a back seat and students who learn to pass tests become more valued than those who do not.

To be sure, there is a great deal of pressure from administrators forcing teachers to improve test scores, so tests have become the classroom's major focus. Teachers jobs sometimes hinge on how their students perform on these tests.

Standardized tests present information that may be biased, unreliable, invalid, and confusing. They do not give any clear indication of a student's future ability. Testing tends to minimize the goals of education and shifts the focus of classroom teaching toward test-taking skills and memorization of facts. Children are being taught information to pass a test that they may forget as soon as their pencils are down.

Standardized tests are machine-scorable instruments that sample performance based on administration over one or (at most) a few days. Standardized test scores are useful in making comparisons among individuals or groups of children at the local, state, and national level. A norm-referenced test (standardized test) is constructed by administering the test to large numbers of students throughout the country in order to develop norms. These norms represent average scores of a sampling of students selected for testing according to their age, sex, race, grade, and socioeconomic status.

Once these norm scores are established, they become the basis for comparing the performance of individuals or groups of children to the performance of the students who were in the norming sample. These comparisons allow you to determine whether a child is making progress or performing in normal ways.

The major purpose of standardized achievement tests is to obtain some indication of how much children have learned. They are used by local school districts, state departments of education, and specific state and federal government programs to assess the "how much" of student achievement in relation to curriculum development and resource allocation. This practice is widespread throughout America.

On reading and literacy tests, the scores from subtests that include, but are not limited to, comprehension, word analysis, and identification are combined to provide a total reading score. Some tests may include a writing piece in response to a wide variety of reading material as part of the test battery.

These tests are general in nature and offer very limited information for instructional planning. These tests can only provide a general idea of a child's reading achievement and may or may not reflect exactly what he or she has learned.

Arguably these tests are mainly measures of intelligence and do not assess what we normally think of as "reading." The tests are plainly unrealistic. Seldom in the real world would someone read a short passage and then be required to answer a series of tricky, convoluted questions about the content. How many people do you see reading a book on the bus who stop to take notes or answer questions?

Tests simply cannot account for the how and the why of a child's reading and writing processing. Standardized tests may also include items closely related to items used to measure intelligence, so they reflect factors other than the effectiveness of reading/literacy instruction.

Because the scores are based on norm groups, they tell little about a child's literacy achievement unless the students in the norm groups are accurately defined and have characteristics similar to that student. There is also the possibility of misinterpreting scores by teachers and parents that can have devastating effects.

Lately there has been a great deal of pressure to achieve high test scores, which can corrupt standardized tests. Each test can only sample specific areas of student achievement. Direct teaching of test-related items in these areas, or what might be called "teaching to the test," can make test results an invalid measure of total student achievement.

For a test to be really reliable and not corrupted by "teaching to the test" strategies, standardized tests are used to provide some assurance of the comparability of results. But this assumes that the reading test a child takes is administered the same way, in the same time of school year, as for the norm group, and that a student has the same characteristics as others within the norm group.

But test scores are subject to a significant error of measurement. Group tests can measure group achievement with some accuracy but do not necessarily measure the achievement of an individual child. Yet we know that standardized tests are frequently used to assess and place individual students.

Test results are best used as one piece of information that is combined with a teacher's alternative forms of assessment such as classroom observations, portfolio assessment, surveys, inventories, checklists, questionnaires, peer reviews, and teacher-made tests. A complete picture of a child's progress and instructional needs should come from such varied forms of assessment.

This said, we can expect standardized tests to be around for a long time. But educators should not ignore the vital connection between the home and school environments that can promote positive test results.

Parents must go the extra mile to assure that their child is getting the right kind of education. Forming a solid connection with your child's teacher is critical. Ask the teacher for the best time to communicate with them via phone. Ask for their email address for after-school discussions. Find out about individual websites where teacher and school postings appear such as class notes and daily homework assignments. Ask about what books are used for reading instruction and for supplemental instruction as well.

Moreover, find out when writing occurs during the daily routines. Ask to see a sample of your child's work and inquire as to how you can help improve your child's performance Ask about how well stocked the classroom is with a wide variety of fiction and non-fiction books. There should be a good balance as well as an adequate amount to encourage independent reading. Ask about how technology is used in your child's class to support reading achievement.

"If you don't ask, you won't get," said my uncle. So true.

Chapter Two

Understanding the New Standards

Standards are what students should learn and be able to accomplish at a certain grade level. Standards are defined as a set of basic and specific learning skills and behaviors that all of our students should strive to achieve. Educators across the country feel that when standards are taught and learned, literacy is fostered which can lead to success in college and beyond.

All states have expectations from children in kindergarten to young adults in high school in, among other disciplines, the language arts. Recently, a new initiative has been undertaken at standardization because our country is concerned with closing the wide gap in achievement within the United States as compared with foreign countries.

Our government feels that our students must raise their literacy standards in order to better compete with other students globally, to succeed in college, and to become competent industrious workers and members of our society.

New standards now exist to further ensure what children should learn at each grade level so they can achieve success now and later on in life as well as to being able to compete with other students in the United States and around the world. These new standards are known as the Common Core State Standards (CCSS). The CCSS effort was launched in 2009 through a partnership of the Council of Chief State School Officers and the National Governors Association which worked together with parents, teachers, school administrators, and educational experts within the United States. A complete version of the standards was published in 2010.

The Common Core State Standards for language arts are comprised of reading, writing, listening, and speaking skills. But states have the right to add their own separate set of educational standards as an addendum to the Common Core Standards. Most states have adopted the CCSS. Some have not.

To further understand your state's standards parents should go to your state's education department standards website. Large cities will have their own standards website. Standards also exist for other disciplines such as math and science.

Even though it is impossible to quantify and identify every behavioral objective in the universe that a child must know and learn, common, across the board standards can help parents fully understand what is expected for their child per grade year.

In addition, parents are now in a better position to hold their local school officials accountable for teaching their children in methods that best support the new standards.

Teachers can also do their fair share of communicating with parents by issuing monthly newsletters updating information about the testing program, among other things that are going on in the classroom.

Open school night, for instance, can be geared to discussions about the standards and testing. Teachers can set up activities for parents when they visit, such as conducting "Make-It and Take-It" reading activities that can be utilized with their students at home. This activity can augment the mundane review of test scores and portfolios which is the usual agenda during Open School night.

Teachers can reach out via phone calls, emails, letters, etc. Just make sure that your administrator is aware of and approves of these initiatives. Seek out your building principal's help in this domain. Teachers can also give out their email address or create their own website for parents to log into.

In addition, teachers should keep parents abreast of the latest reading techniques and strategies by supplying them with handy websites such as Scholastic.com for helpful reading/writing ideas.

Finally, once a year, hold a Read-A-Thon whereby parents and students are invited to the classroom on a Saturday morning and partake in various literacy events and activities which would include refreshments, games, prizes, etc.

IDEA BANK

- Keep the lines of communication open with your child's teachers and principals.
- If you do not understand something, say something.
- Familiarize yourself with your state's process and procedures of standardized testing.

Chapter Three

Parents Can Make the Difference

It is a well-known fact that parents can and do make a difference in helping their children become strategic, competent readers. That is why this book attempts to instill in parents a modicum of expertise in order to provide explicit and direct reading instruction in the areas of word identification, vocabulary development, and reading comprehension. They can also help their children increase scores on reading tests by assuming the role of literacy coach at home.

Parents can do positive things to advance these goals such as:

- talk to their child's teachers and principals
- form focus groups with other parents to discuss testing procedures
- become more involved in parent-teacher associations
- attend school board meetings
- talk to your child

The state standards are too numerous to mention specifically. They can be quite confusing to both teachers and parents, but in terms of teaching reading objectives, the standards require that children apply a more critical lens in their understanding of authentic and sophisticated reading material. The tests ask that children become more strategic readers in that they must be able to interpret a wide variety of fiction and non-fiction, including poetry, letters, articles, etc.

Also, writing skills that children are asked to demonstrate on standardized tests are expected to relate to how well your child can write and address specific writing tasks including but not limited to arguments, informational/explanatory texts, and narratives. Also included are rubrics which are concerned with gauging writing organization and grammar, as well as the effective use of vocabulary in writing.

Speaking and listening skills, although they may not actually be an objective of the current crop of objective testing, are nevertheless a requirement that your child must show as they learn to develop a broad range of pragmatic oral communication skills.

In addition to parents coaching the reading/writing process at home, teachers can contribute to this effort by helping parents gain the skills and strategies needed to help their children. Among these strategies is to help parents become aware of the type and nature of the standardized testing requirements and procedures conducted by their local school districts and by state directives.

Teachers must reach out to parents to build bridges of knowledge and trust in order to facilitate success at home and at school. In addition to standardized tests, parents should also be made and become cognizant in other forms of reading tests, such as diagnostic and placement tests given by either the on-site reading specialist or the classroom teacher.

It is necessary for both parents and teachers to address the CCSS by attempting to do the following:

1. Read equal amounts of fiction and non-fiction.
2. Explore all genres of reading and writing.
3. Focus on daily reading of newspapers, local and national. My smartest friends always read the newspapers and kept asking questions to their other friends. They would say: "Did you hear what happened to . . . ?" When we couldn't answer, we knew we were at a deficit. Literacy is knowledge. Are we teaching our children properly? Will they remember what happened on December 7, 1941, or June 6, 1944? Will they know what happened on September 11, 2001? I hope so.

Teachers can specifically encourage children on a daily basis to communicate freely in the open classroom in a free, honest, and open exchange of ideas. It is also necessary to build schema or background knowledge before reading anything using family situations, videos, trips, the Internet, etc. Talk "up" to children using higher vocabulary to instill thought and interest. Use word walls for content specific lessons.

Teachers should allow for a wide variety of opportunities at reading to, with, and by your students. Have your students write every day especially in response to what they are reading. Work with your students on an individual basis as well as in cooperative partnerships, and in small groups.

In addition to testing, teachers must be able to gather sufficient information about each and every student. This can be done with classroom observation; parent, teacher, and student conferencing; informal note taking; teacher monitoring guidebooks; specific reading checklists; and the use of rubrics or criteria scoring mini-assessments to evaluate writing skills.

Rubrics serve to guide children as well as parents in their quest for competence in writing. Rubrics identify what a valuable, viable piece of writing is comprised of and what is lacking in quality of a specific writing piece. They show what can be an excellent product or a poor one and at various levels and stages in-between.

But the best rubric is the one a teacher develops step by step with their students and is used in the daily writing process.

IDEA BANK

- Become familiar with your state's Common Core Standards.
- Ask whether these standards are directly tied to the standardized tests given annually.
- Identify those writing skills and accompanying rubrics used to gauge those skills.

Chapter Four

What to Expect Students Will Encounter on a Standardized Test

Schools all across America are required to administer standardized tests to students in grades 3–8. This guidebook covers only school grades 3, 4, and 5. These tests monitor children's progress and determine whether or not they are reading below, on, or above grade level.

However, there exists a controversy over whether a teacher should "teach to the test." Should the test drive instruction? Or should good teaching practices and routines be maintained despite whatever testing procedures are in place. Teachers are caught between a rock and a hard place. They want to be creative, but does their creativity become stifled because of these rigorous testing parameters? They know they are being held accountable. Their jobs may be at risk.

Usually teachers are dictated to from school administrators, principals, and district language arts coordinators and consultants. They inevitably evoke a "Do as I say" mantra which negates teacher individualism, motivation, and personal initiative. It will stifle creativity. Teachers invariably then plan an inordinate amount of time, usually from September to April, for test preparation then can neglect language arts for the rest of the term because the pressure is off.

We have witnessed that tests produce student, teacher, administrator, and parent anxiety. Since building principals can assess at a glance what an individual's test scores are, could we then assume that these results can be used to determine a teacher's worth vis-á-vis tenure or re-hiring? Yet, what's the difference? Teachers, parents, and children have no choice but to become familiar with the standardized test format, learn test-taking strategies, and do a voluminous amount of time-consuming practice tests.

To measure achievement in reading and writing, and in other subjects for that matter, each school district across America usually adopts a different standardized test to use for evaluation. It is next to impossible to know exactly what would be required on any given test, but generally there is a format that's common to all.

Teachers administer tests to large groups in a classroom. These tests are usually scored electronically but can be hand scored. Testing may be done in a single sitting in one day but most likely occurs in multiple sittings or sessions over two or three days. The test is timed, which may be neither helpful nor fair to students who require extra time to answer questions completely and accurately.

The homeroom teacher proctors the test, but there are special testing conditions for children with special needs who require modifications. Children can be moved to a smaller location where they are monitored closely. Teachers can only read directions, hand out pencils, and post the time parameters on the blackboard. They may not read a question or explain or help a child obtain the answer in any manner, with possible exceptions as governed by modified conditions granted to special-education students.

Tests might ask for the meaning of vocabulary, including antonyms, synonyms, or picking out words in context. Tests sometimes incorporate a read-aloud piece where the teacher reads a story twice and children merely listen, take notes, and respond by planning and writing about different aspects of the story. For such read-aloud passages, the text of the actual story students listen to is not given to them.

Another section of the test may be short answer/multiple-choice questions. These questions usually ask penetrating and probing types of questions of the higher-order thinking kind. These types of questions can make an easy story difficult to comprehend. They are not as easy as "Who was buried in Grant's Tomb?" (if you know what I mean).

Questions that are asked of children involve deep thinking, not just on their basic knowledge and understanding of the text, but also on application, analysis, synthesis, and evaluation. Inferential questions, predictive questions, and summative questions are asked. Some of the answers can be mined directly from the text; some might have to be further studied as a student "reads between the lines" (in other words, the answers are not exactly there on the page).

Some answers are not in the given text at all and require students to use their knowledge, expectations of the topic, and past experiences to draw a viable conclusion or to interpret what the author's point of view seems to be. Questions involving two selections are sometimes given where a student must refer back to text A and compare and contrast that with text B that is similar in nature.

Reading standardized tests may measure and contain, but are not limited to, a wide variety of subskills such as drawing inferences about characters, drawing conclusions about events; identifying story elements using evidence from stories to describe characters; determining meaning of unfamiliar words by using context clues; identifying the main idea and supporting details of a passage; locating information in a text to solve a problem; analyzing ideas based on prior knowledge and personal experiences; discriminating among a variety of texts; using specific evidence to identify themes; using key vocabulary to interpret stories; using graphic organizers; using knowledge of story structure; analyzing ideas based on prior knowledge and personal experiences; and evaluating the content by identifying the author's purpose.

Tests have come a long way. They are more specific, more exacting, and less superficial than just asking the five *w*'s and *h* type questions (who, what, when, where, why, and how).

A sample test day might look like this:

The first session can involve answering questions from a passage that might be fiction or non-fiction; it may be a letter, poem, diary, interview, simulated news article, want ad, or fairy tale. The test may ask students to compare and contrast two letters written by the same person or by different people writing about the same topic. Students may have to answer from passages that relate to one another or promote opposing viewpoints.

Questions are usually multiple-choice, with four choices given and only one correct response, although some of the responses may be almost correct. Sometimes it is helpful to teach about what we call the process of elimination to arrive at the best and most valid response. There may be as many as thirty questions given.

The second session may involve listening comprehension. In this case, a selection is read aloud twice to students. Students must listen carefully since they do not have a hard copy of the passage to refer to. They will be asked to plan and respond to the story they have just heard, perhaps in the form of interpreting a question or statement. Students may also be asked to write some form of personal response related to the main idea or theme of the story. Writing is usually scored by a rubric that focuses on how clearly students organized and expressed their ideas, how accurately and completely they answered the questions, how well they supported their ideas with examples, how interesting and enjoyable their writing was, and how correctly they used grammar, spelling, punctuation, and paragraphs.

Students may be required to take notes while they are listening to the passage. Note taking is a critical skill that is taught in school and can be reinforced at home. Children might be asked to complete a graphic organizer using details they heard from the story.

A graphic organizer is used to help students extract and identify pertinent points of information in a passage and as an aid to comprehension and a guide for writing. It can come in many shapes and sizes requiring a student to, for instance, identify the main idea in a passage and list specific details. It can look something like this:

MAIN IDEA

Detail #1   Detail #2   Detail #3
List   List   List

Students may also be asked to use information they heard in the story to write a conclusion or create an inference or interpret the end of the story. Children must learn to answer in complete sentences, use the wording from the question, and turn it into the beginning of the response.

For example, a question might read, "Why did Jeremy get sick after eating the pizza?" The student's answer should read, "Jeremy got sick after eating the pizza because _____." This is called a structured response to a story question. If the test calls for a five-line response, encourage pupils to write five lines. Anything less might be construed by test evaluators (who are usually other teachers within the district but not a child's teacher nor any other teacher within the same school) as inferior, garnering fewer points. A question for which a longer response is expected might read, "Explain how and why Erica's luck changes a few times in this story." In the answer, a student would be asked to respond to and include various points that must be addressed:

1. Tell how Erica's luck starts before school.
2. Describe how Erica's luck changes when she gets to school.
3. Explain how and why Erica's luck changes by the end of the story.
4. Use details from the story in your answer.

The test will instruct students to check their writing to correct spelling, grammar, capitalization, and punctuation.

If the writing question calls for thirty lines of composition (these lines are printed on the page and are usually double-spaced), then students must answer completely, using up to the thirty-line limit to ensure a maximum number of points. Even if they answer completely and thoroughly, with, let's say, ten lines of discourse, test evaluators may take this to mean that the answer is incomplete.

In this case, it certainly is better to be safe than sorry. Some responses are shorter and only call for a written answer of five lines. The same rule applies. More in this case might be better, but just give them what they want—no more, no less.

Another part of a writing test may require an extended response that involves students writing their own compositions about a given topic, possibly based on the story just read or on prior experiences. Students will first be asked to plan a response on a separate planning page.

The next task will be to write a story about a topic, such as making a new friend. For example, "Describe how you met, what you did the first day together, and what helped you become friends."

Students will be prompted to include the following items:

1. Write a title for your story.
2. Write a clear beginning, middle, and end to the story.
3. Write specific details to make your story interesting.

Once again, test evaluators will be looking for correct spelling, grammar, capitalization, and punctuation. These items will be marked via rubric (see Table 15.1 for a sample writing rubric, p. 83). Students must address all points asked for in order to obtain full credit.

Each paragraph in the extended response section must include a topic sentence that tells the main idea of the paragraph. It must also contain supportive sentences that give facts, ideas, and examples that support the main idea or topic sentence. There should be some type of "clincher" sentence at the end of each paragraph that closes off and concludes the paragraph by restating the main idea in different terms. A student should remember these pointers:

- Did I indent my first sentence?
- Did I spell each word correctly?
- Did I provide capitals, periods, and commas where needed?

While writing their compositions, students should stop periodically, maybe every other paragraph, and ask themselves the following questions:

Am I answering the question they want me to answer? Am I proving my point of view or my topic sentence? Does what I am writing make sense? Am I including all the bulleted points the test question calls for? Am I fully and completely answering the question with an appropriate length?

In session three, students may be asked to read a passage by themselves and fill in a graphic organizer. Graphic organizers are very useful in helping students learn to organize and analyze ideas. Organizers can be used to support students as they read, study, take notes, and plan products and in a variety of other facets of learning. They will be asked to read a passage and respond by filling out a graphic organizer that may look something like this:

THREE THINGS THAT SHOW DOLPHINS ARE SMART

Response #1   Response #2   Response #3

Students may be asked to organize a written response based on the information gathered within the graphic organizer. They may then be asked to read another story and supply short answers to questions about the story. They will be asked to use information from the story to support their answers. In addition, students may be asked to write a letter or journal entry as another task related to the story. The possibilities are endless.

Standardized tests will be administered in many different formats and will be different for every school district throughout the United States depending upon what company developed the test, which one had the testing parameters favorable to a school district, and how affordable it is for the particular district.

A building principal should hold a series of meetings in advance of the test to clarify all of the above items. If necessary, parents should request a meeting with the principal, teacher, or reading specialist to address any concerns.

A parent should inquire about these technical points by writing these questions down on a notepad while asking a teacher and/or administrator:

1. What is the name of the test?
2. When is the test given?
3. How many days will it take?
4. Who will administer the test?
5. How will it be marked?
6. Are there special testing modifications and conditions in place should my child need them?
7. How can I help my child prepare?
8. What grades are taking the test?
9. Will my child be given a makeup test if he or she is excused due to illness or emotional reasons, or is absent for some other reason?
10. What does the test cover?
11. When I get the results, who will help me interpret the scores?
12. Is the test given in languages besides English?

Test items will vary in type and structure. As mentioned above, students may be given passages from stories or novels, nonfiction, letters, fairy tales, science, social studies, history, interviews, poetry, informational articles, biographies, fables, geography, world history, magazine articles, newspaper articles, autobiographies, mysteries, web pages from

Internet sites, memoirs, cookbooks, politics, or from virtually any other legitimate source.

Some tests are geared to test only word recognition, reading vocabulary, and reading comprehension in a simple multiple-choice format without any writing component. Educators and parents must know ahead of time the exact format of the test.

IDEA BANK

Here is one final set of questions parents should remember to ask:

1. How will my child's teacher effectively prepare him/her for this test?
2. Are there practice tests and practice sessions given by the school and district?
3. Will my child be familiar with developing guidelines and learning strategies to develop cogent writing responses, fill out graphic organizers, and utilize various genres and reading strategies to unlock the meaning of the sample passages?

Parents should ask plenty of questions. Remember, the only stupid question is the one never asked. The more informed parents are, the more effective they can be.

Chapter Five

Taking Another Look

Some states that have adopted the Common Core State Standards are offering high stakes assessments in English Language Arts (ELA) that correlate to these new standards.

As of this writing, only two states in the nation administer tests aligned with the Common Core standards which forty-five states have adopted. Yet all states have some form of standardized test in language arts to conform with state requirements. Even though these tests should not be considered an absolute and definitive assessment of a child's reading ability, they are still being given. The pressure is on and anxiety levels are high.

For instance, New York City and New York State began in the spring of 2013 to administer a language arts test based directly on Common Core Standards for grades 3–8. If this is indicative of a new trend, and it very well may be, other states will follow suit.

As a resource for parents and teachers, New York State maintains a website for their revised testing program. Their website involves two parts: An educator guide to the ELA test for grades 3–8 which outlines the overview and synopsis and rationale of the test, what's involved, scope and sequence, and implementation procedures. The other part of the testing packet of materials involves an ELA Common Core Sample Questions guidebook.

Since this guidebook is limited to the elementary grades, parents and teachers should become familiar with grades 3–5 protocols.

Here is an overview of what the test covers for grades 3–5 reflecting newly embedded items from Common Core standards.

GRADE THREE: READING, WRITING, AND LANGUAGE

In this newly revised test, speaking and listening skills were not assessed. But keep in mind that many other states may still test these skills. All passages were authentic and hopefully interesting to read. The sample items were all excerpted from the original text. Authentic means it was written by a valid and noted author and not by some unknown freelance writer of children's test materials.

Nevertheless, who knows what our students will encounter. Even passages from famous authors may be difficult to decipher because their use of language is not controlled by the publishers of the test themselves. In addition, some text selections will express opinions from authentic writers which students may find disagreeable.

Text passages are longer and more challenging. ELA test booklets are divided into four sub-test books to be administered over a daunting three day consecutive period. Maximum testing times have changed and new rubrics to score short and extended answers to questions have been developed. We should understand that guidelines vary from state to state but the essence of the testing remains the same.

Reading—Day One—Book One—Five Passages—Thirty multiple choice questions—Seventy minutes to complete. Phew!

Passages on this portion of the test will be taken from original author works that are found in books, etc. Students will be asked to read these passages exploring an author's opinion, purpose, and point of view. Students also will have to ascertain whether arguments presented are valid or specious and why.

Some questions will demand that students look back to the text to glean their answers so they may be factually based. Skimming and scanning for facts can be taught which will help children.

A child can erase an answer and choose another, but the first selection unless absolutely and obviously wrong, should be left alone. First instincts are the best instincts. Some questions will relate to the behavior of main characters whereby students must select the right kind of descriptive adjectives. So teaching characterization, that is how characters behave, act, think, and say, is critical.

Sometimes there might be questions about the setting of a story; where a story takes place. But stories can have multiple settings. Teach how to map a multiple plot story. Also discuss time, clock time, calendar time, place or places, and whether the story takes place in the past, present, or future and what items in the story tell the reader that. A settings map is simply a road map that children draw and label that depicts where the characters have been, what they've done and where they are going, and what they're doing next.

Questions about vocabulary can be derived through contextual analysis, or figures of speech such as similes and metaphors may help to uncover meaning through deciphering highly descriptive and sophisticated language an author uses.

So your child may be given a fictional passage to consider, such as a fairy tale or fable, and then have it paired with, that is to be contrasted and compared to, an informational work in science or social studies. Therefore, reading to your child should always reflect authentic fiction, non-fiction, and poetry. Paying important attention to details and facts is critical. A child should synthesize, analyze, draw conclusions, and learn to eliminate extraneous and irrelevant information.

Reading—Day Two—More passages and multiple choice questions

And in addition, passages that require a short written response to questions based on the passage as well as extended response questions will also be included.

The multiple choice question section asks for students to analyze different aspects of the selected sample text which involves, but is not limited to, questions involving main idea, characterization, plot and setting, and key vocabulary. Questions seem to require a simple recall of facts less and less. We see a demand to extract from the student deeper thinking on multiple levels. Also multiple test choices are thrown in to confuse or lead the student to choose not the best answer, but a distorted, non-verifiable answer. Children must be very savvy and discerning and should not allow themselves into being "tricked" into settling for a mediocre answer. Confusing? You bet!

Reading—Day Two—Fifty minutes—Short and extended response questions

The next task is for students to read other passages, possibly a folktale or fairytale, and respond to them by answering questions using written statements usually indicating two details from the story that prove your child's answer. Your child must write in complete, cohesive, and coherent sentences. These questions are geared to have the student draw conclusions based on evidence, make a judgment, or devise an opinion.

These short sentence responses are graded using a short response rubric indicating that a certain amount of points will be given by virtue of the length and adequacy of the written response. Clear, concise, valid, and relevant sentences receive the most points.

Responses that are deemed irrelevant because they fail to address the questions directive or objective will either get fewer or no points. Your child must provide the necessary evidentiary retort in a coherent, intelligent, and an intelligible way.

Some errors in grammar and sentence structure are allowed as long as they do not debilitate from the overall meaning of the response. Yet comprehension of these passages is key. Without gleaning meaning, a child's written response will inevitably be inadequate and weak. Reading comprehension and writing skills go hand in hand.

Day Three

Day Two as well as Day Three call for, in addition to short response sentences, the need to produce extended written responses. From the same or different passages, which again may be fictional or non-fictional in nature, the extended response will also require a student to completely understand the passage and then compose not short sentences, but a full length essay-type response. The task will demand that your child express an opinion, take a stand on some issue, and support that opinion with facts and details from within the text.

What is required is a completely coherent, well developed, and defined essay with well thought out and clearly written structures. Each paragraph should have a clearly defined topic sentence with accompanying details to support the topic sentence and a relevant concluding sentence.

So what they want is a child to develop a good introductory paragraph. Good supporting "body" paragraphs, and a concluding paragraph which sums everything up and ties it all together. This is a precursor to college essay writing and that is what they want the students to start preparing to learn how to do.

A writing rubric or scale is used to judge the significance and competence of the written work. Exemplary writing is seen as using complex ideas and facts and information that are excised from the story in order to support the thesis or topic. Evidence from the story must be used to support the topic. Even quoting from the primary source may be required. Organization of the essay, that is having a beginning, middle, and end, will be noted as well as competently using correct grammar, sentence structure, and spelling.

This writing in response to literature must be well thought out and expository in nature. Merely relating a personal narrative in explication is not called for and will not garner enough points to pass.

Grades 4–5 follow similar routines. But it behooves both parents and teachers to become thoroughly familiar with their state's test format and requirements. Schools can help parents understand, but parents must go the extra mile to assure that they know exactly what their children must know and be made aware of.

IDEA BANK

Don't wait a month before test day to familiarize yourself with the test's structure. Start in the summer or at least the early fall to determine what is required.

Chapter Six

The Flip Side of Testing

As with all standardized testing, there are drawbacks. First parents may have difficulty in extracting and understanding information about assessments from their local schools. Remember what my uncle said: "If you don't ask, you won't get." Simple enough, huh! If you are not aggressive in your search for answers from your school officials and teachers, you won't get any. That's how schools work.

You have to be an advocate for your child and stand up for his or her rights. In some cases teachers may not know themselves what is expected. They feel that, and rightly so, they want to teach the whole child and not the mundane obligatory information required on state assessments. Their passion for teaching is diminished in view of the current obsession with testing. Teachers feel they aren't given enough time nor possess adequate materials to correctly implement the test properly and to provide positive pre-test skills for their students.

Then, there is anxiety to cope with. The only way to reduce it would be to support and encourage your child as well as become familiar with what is known and what will be predictable about the test format.

Despite the fact that your child is expected to meet or exceed Common Core grade level expectations, parents and teachers must be cognizant of what those expectations or benchmarks are for their children. Teachers, parents, and some researchers, some of whom feel that these tests are not designed to measure true growth in reading skills, have not been able to influence the current trends in assessment.

Are these tests, instead of determining reading achievement, being used to unfairly and inequitably label students as well as to inaccurately measure teaching competence and effectiveness?

Teachers, and even to a lesser extent parents, may have somewhat of a voice in high stakes testing, but is anybody really listening?

IDEA BANK

In coping with worry and test anxiety, be calming, soothing, and supportive to your child. Offer words of encouragement and love.

Chapter Seven

A Quiet Place

Parents should set up a quiet study area at home. This could include a home library with a special bookshelf housing a wide variety of literary genre, DVDs, cassettes with books, and magazines. Some books can be bought as alternatives to the standard holiday items, and some can be purchased at the local mall bookstore, through the Internet, or from school-based book clubs. The room should have no phones, no food, no games, no music, and no TV. Sitting on a bed does not promote good posture, so have a child use a comfortable chair.

Develop and post a schedule for the children to follow: this should include time for doing homework and studying, the time for help with homework can be given, and the time allowed for watching television and other recreation. Also post an alphabet chart like the ones in school. They can be purchased from teacher supply stores, or (even better) create one with your child with pictures, words, and sentences. Parents should also have a chart with newly learned words that they can refer to when reading the current story.

An additional venue for quiet reading could be the public library or a bookstore where seating and tables are available. Many are now outfitted with snack bars and restaurants that offer healthy foods. This may break the monotony of doing the program in the same room at the same time every day. Natural settings like backyards, parks, playgrounds, or even at the beach may offer new challenges to reading. Don't forget to stock your car with cassette tapes and books for those long and arduous trips during summer vacation or when paying a visit to Grandma.

Many schools sponsor Read-Ins or Read-A-Thons. Parents can sponsor a sleepover Read-A-Thon where friends sleep over; along with the usual

TEXTBOX 7.1 READING INTEREST INVENTORY

1. What is the name of your favorite book that someone has read aloud to you?
2. What is the name of your favorite book that you have read for yourself?
3. What kind of stories and books do you like to hear read aloud to you?
4. What sections of the library do you like?
5. What are the names of your favorite television programs?
6. Do you read the comics in the newspapers?
7. What do you really like to do at school?
8. What is your favorite computer game?
9. What do you really like to do on a Saturday?
10. What kinds of games do you play with your friends? When you are alone?
11. Do you have a favorite hobby?
12. Do you enjoy reading for fun or do you read only because of school?

games, guests bring books to share and read to each other. Seek suggestions from your child's teacher.

In order to help you stock the room with appropriate material, a parent may want to administer a general Reading Interest Inventory by asking a series of questions that can be answered orally or in written form. A sample inventory is shown in textbox 7.1. In addition, throughout the school year, students should keep track of books read by filling in a chart (table 7.1) by genre.

A quiet place offers a good beginning, but other factors are equally important. Make sure children are given good nutritious meals. See that they exercise daily as well. It is also important that students get sufficient rest. Parents should allow for a modicum of extracurricular school activities, too, but do not overload.

Table 7.1. Books I Have Read So Far

Animals and Nature	Sports	Mysteries/Adventure
Science Fiction	Humor	Modern Fiction
Myths, Legends, Fables	Poetry	Biography/Autobiography
Historical Fiction	History	Other/Miscellaneous

IDEA BANK

Set up a quiet, peaceful place in your home without all the electronic influences where your child can think and study without undue interference.

Chapter Eight

Pinpoint Reading Overview
Review—Read—Reinforce—Retell

What can lead to greater success for your child is a program called *Pinpoint Reading*. Each session takes only twenty minutes. It is a program that offers review, reinforcement, and retelling where a child reads aloud while parents listen and discuss what was read. This is a wonderful opportunity for parents to get involved in a child's world of books and to help reinforce learning in a positive and rewarding way. This should be an enjoyable time for everyone, so the emphasis is not on strict or direct instruction, but on simply reading for pleasure with a few added activities that are fast-paced and keep the time interesting.

Pinpoint Reading is designed to provide educators and parents with the know-how to enhance a child's reading and writing ability and to encourage a love and respect for reading. It describes and emphasizes certain strategies that can be used to help children become better readers and thereby significantly increase their scores on standardized tests in reading and other academic areas as well.

When introducing a book, begin by having children look at the front and back cover and discuss what they see, including any blurbs, summaries, and reviews. They can read the inside introduction. Find the part of the book that gives a short summary. Do they know anything about the author? Discuss the table of contents to find out what the book is all about. Take a picture walk by looking at and discussing the illustrations and how the pictures are portrayed. Did the author do his or her own drawings? Look at the size of the print and the length of the book. Have they seen the movie version of the story? Have they heard the music or songs based on the book?

As you listen to children read aloud, talk about what you enjoy or find interesting. Try to relate the material to their life experiences. Ask them what part of the story they enjoyed the most. Ask what they think will happen next, before turning the page.

Children usually pick the books, but they may need assistance. To determine whether a book is appropriately leveled, use the section below.

HOW TO CHOOSE A BOOK
THAT IS RIGHT FOR YOUR CHILD

Have a child browse, skim, scan, and compare books. He or she can preview the book first by reading the title and chapter titles to get a sense of what kind of book it is and what it is all about. The child should decide if the topic or genre of the book is interesting enough. Then skim and scan the first few paragraphs of the first chapter to see if the author captures a child's interest right away.

The book may be too easy if:

1. The book flows too easily.
2. The ideas are simple and easy to understand.
3. The words do not get in the way.

The book may be just right if:

1. Most of the ideas are understood.
2. Some of the words are unknown, but the child can figure them out or pass them by.

The book may be too challenging if:

1. It is too difficult to read.
2. Understanding the main ideas is difficult.
3. Understanding a lot of the action or events in the story is too hard.
4. The words are too hard.

The types of books to have on hand should include, but are not limited to, biography, fiction, nonfiction, historical fiction, fantasy, poetry, myths,

TEXTBOX 8.1 MY READING RECORD

My Own Evaluation and Comments
Book Title_____ Date Started/Finished_____/_____
For each question below, answer Yes or No.
Liked book?
Disliked book?
Interesting book?
Boring book?
Book too easy?
Book too hard?
Want more books like this?
Interested in subject matter?
Would recommend to others?

legends, fables, letters, and magazines. To further help with the selection, a short bibliography has been included that can be found in chapter 20.

It's a good idea to keep track of the progress of the program by marking off on a wall calendar each day parents and children have read together for the twenty-minute period. You can add to the calendar some free-reading days where children choose optional material to read such as a comic book, a computer-assisted book, a cassette tape, a newspaper, a magazine, or even some baseball cards.

Keep the atmosphere positive. Let children know that you think it is great when they read with expression and intonation, attempt a difficult word, or read smoothly with adequate fluency. It is a well-known fact that children learn to read by reading every day. You cannot learn to swim if you don't get into the pool.

It's always a good idea to ask children to make predictions before, during, and after they have read something. Predicting is a critical reading comprehension strategy. Sharing what might happen next in a story also motivates children and makes them want to read on.

Discuss the book so children can better understand what they have read. Talk about the setting, characters, problems, and solutions. Sometimes you can have a child answer questions in writing or just talk about the literature.

Discuss and review interesting vocabulary. Relate the new vocabulary to something in their lives or something they have seen on television or in the movies.

Children should keep an active, ongoing, evaluative log of all the books read during the school year. A sample log is given in textbox 8.1.

The next section gives the specific schedule and procedure for Pinpoint Reading.

THE PINPOINT READING PROGRAM

Parents should implement this program on a daily basis every evening including (and I'll leave this to your discretion) weekends and holidays. The program requires a twenty-minute intensive workout. The workout is fast-paced and should be time-restricted. If you cannot finish, continue the next day but do not go over the time limitations. It is critical to discuss the importance of the program, its goals and objectives, and why you want to have your child involved in this program. It is equally important to ask the child what he or she wants to see happen and to articulate his or her own personal goals. You may wish to develop a contract with your child stating mutually agreeable goals of the program, listing the requirements and procedures, and a pledge to work at achieving those goals. The specific procedures are outlined below:

- Step 1: Review Previously Read Material, three minutes
- Step 2: Predictive Writing Journal, two minutes
- Step 3: Pinpoint Reading—Reinforce (Vocabulary/Understanding), ten minutes
- Step 4: Retell Material, Read Journal (Personal Response), five minutes
- Total program = twenty minutes

Let's begin.

Step 1: Review previously read material (three minutes)

The following are suggested focal points for reviewing the previous day's work. It is not necessary to complete all points within the three-minute time frame.

- Briefly review the elements of the story read so far by having the student recall the story title, characters, setting, problem, and any solutions.
- Discuss important events or any new and important words learned.
- Ask for a short summary by asking, "So far, what are some of the things that have happened in the story or have happened to the characters?"
- Students can read from previous entries from their reading logs to refresh their memories.
- Ask if they have any questions about what they have read so far.
- Have them read a paragraph or two from the previous chapter or section to check for fluency and expression.
- Ask if they have any difficulties with the plot, new information, or vocabulary.
- If no previous story exists, skip to Step 2.

TEXTBOX 8.2 PREDICTIVE WRITING JOURNAL

Story Title: _____

Author: _____

Illustrator: _____

My Story Predictions: _____

_____

_____

_____

_____

_____

_____

Step 2: Predictive writing journal—one sentence (two minutes)

- Keep a writing journal, diary, or log for children to write in every night.
- Ask them to write just one complete sentence predicting what will happen next based on your discussion of the previously read material.
- You may ask them to look at the pictures in the next part of the book to elicit responses.

- Encourage taking educated guesses and accept almost any legitimate relevant response.
- Make sure that proper writing structures are followed.
- Encourage children to speak in full sentences and write in full sentences as well.
- Model the correction of any errors on the spot after they are done writing, but let them do their own correcting, revising, and editing with your help.
- A short, simple format for a predictive writing journal is shown in Textbox 8.2.

Step 3: Pinpoint Reading—Reinforce challenging vocabulary and understanding of text (ten minutes)

This portion of the workout is critical. It is separated into two sections:

Section A: Before-Reading Activity—Preparation

The following steps will help a parent begin to prepare for reading a book:

- Before your child reads the book he or she chose, explain that he or she will be reading aloud to you so that you will be able to learn where the child's strengths and weaknesses are.
- First discuss the book cover and title, the author's life, the illustrator, and the back cover, and review any book flaps.
- Then model a sample sentence to show how to read aloud with expression. Ham it up. Be an actor. Show your child how to bring words to life and make them powerful.

Section B: During Reading—Steps in the Pinpoint Reading Process

Step B-1
- Ask the child to begin reading aloud the first couple of sentences, up to one paragraph.
- Correct any mistakes on the spot by asking the child to try to sound out any troublesome words.

- When the child meets a tricky word, he or she can think about what the story is about, check the picture to get a hint, go back, and try to sound it out.
- The child can look for chunks in the word—for example, find the smaller parts like *on* as in the word *onward*, look for word endings such as *-ing* or *-ly*, or find little words in compound words like *maybe* or *tonight*.
- If a mistake is made as the child reads, remind the child to ask him- or herself, "Does that make sense? Would we say it that way? Does it look just right to me?"
- If this does not work, tell the child to keep reading to see if he or she can pick up important contextual clues to help unlock that difficult word. Finding context clues is a strategy for decoding words in which the reader uses the meaning of the surrounding sentences or words as clues to understanding the unknown word.
- Use any available picture to help the child think about the difficult word.
- Allow the child to self-correct as many times as possible.
- Finally, and let this be the last thing you do, say the word and move on. Red-flag this word on a chart or index card for review later.
- Quick-check comprehension and understanding by asking questions at the end of the paragraph or section read such as:
  Is the story making sense so far?
  Can you retell what's happening so far?
  What do you think might happen next?
  Have any of the questions you asked or the ideas you've predicted been answered?
  Are your guesses right or wrong?

Step B-2

- Reinforce the material just read in the paragraph by asking for a re-statement of the main idea of the paragraph, and elicit any important supportive details.
- Reinforce any red-flagged words by asking for repeated pronunciations and word meanings using flash cards of those words written on index cards.

- Repetition here is the key to decoding. Merely unlocking a word once doesn't guarantee safekeeping. A child needs to place these words into his or her mind vault and lock them in forever.
- Make sure the child understands that paragraph before moving to the next passage. I believe in quality, not quantity, when it comes to reading comprehension and word recognition. Rereading builds fluency. Stumbling through text, paragraph after paragraph, without stopping is pointless. If no problems are apparent or if the text has nothing of value, move on.
- Then read the next paragraph.
- That's right: Go slow, be deliberate, even if you just get through a few paragraphs in a given evening. Quality reading time is critical. Take time to make the needed connections.

A word on word banks: Those red-flagged words can be placed on 3 × 5 index cards as needed. On one side of the card, print the word, and have the children create a good sentence using that word that actually explains what the word means on the other side of the card. Keep the cards in a pile and review them daily during the three-minute review section. Try to keep the list of words that are challenging as well as sight words such as *done* or *there*.

Step B-3
- Continue reading paragraph by paragraph.
- Stop often to ask relevant questions.
- You can adjust the flow to prevent boredom. If a child is struggling, stop more often, less often if they are not. But always ask questions. Don't forget the 5 *w*'s and the *h* (*who, what, where, when, why,* and *how*).
- Finish the page and then stop.
- Repeat steps one and two where necessary.
- If the child is doing well, he or she can read some parts silently at other times, but if the story is too easy, then change the book.
- Emphasize the importance of controlling the flow if a child is struggling.
- If necessary, stop more frequently to question and reinforce vocabulary.
- Go back if necessary and repeat the sentence they struggled with, the paragraph that was too difficult, or reinforce the entire page. Then have

the child repeat it again and as many times as necessary in order to gain mastery.

- When a child reads aloud, listen first to any mistakes, giving the child some wait time (several seconds or more), to see if he or she will self-correct. Try to enable the child to read with the tools needed to be an independent, strategic reader and thinker.

> *If you give a child a fish, he will eat.*
> *If you teach him how to fish, he has food forever.*

This strict emphasis on repeated readings of the same material until mastery is achieved is the hallmark of this program and can enable a child to become a more accomplished, independent reader with greater confidence, skill, and fluency. Research has shown that ". . . guided repeated oral reading procedure that included guidance from teachers, peers, or parents had a significant and positive impact on word recognition, fluency, and comprehension across a range of grade levels" (National Institute of Child Health and Human Development, 2000, summary, p. 24).

However, if you think that stopping along the continuum of text is tedious and may lead to a child losing interest, then adjust the length accordingly. Stop at every other paragraph, or stop at the bottom of the page or every other page. But be careful not to overextend the material only because it may lead to a drop in retention as they continue down the page until they finish the passage.

That is why stopping points are a good thing. But if a child is handling the page well, then make adjustments to your interventions. You'd be surprised how much information a child will pick up during the rereading phase. It's the same as wanting to see a movie again because you weren't sure what you actually saw or understood?

Step 4: Retell material read—Journal out personal responses (five minutes)

- At the culmination of the workout, ask for a retelling of the story of what sections were read aloud. This helps build memory and in turn comprehension.

- For the retelling, ask the child to recall in his or her own words the story title, characters, setting, story problem so far, and any solutions.
- The child can also tell the main events of the beginning, middle, and end of the story.
- Ask the child to recall as much information as possible by prompting with questions: tell me more. Prove what you said. How do you know? Or simply ask why.
- Afterward, have the child write a sentence or two in his or her journal about personal reactions to an event, a character, some action, a favorite part of the story, or simply why the child enjoyed or did not enjoy what was read.
- Ask the child to read his or her written response. Share your ideas.

This concludes the workout. The next day pick up where you left off.

If a child becomes tired before the twenty minutes are up, then stop. Should you miss a session or two, you can still pick it up the next day. Continuity and routine is important. Even during vacation and holiday periods, you can still do the program.

But what happens if a parent cannot participate for extended periods of time? A sibling or other relative can step in. At the risk of sounding silly, the child can even read to a pet if necessary, or a favorite doll or action figure. You can also rely on cassette tapes with accompanying texts. A child can listen to prerecorded stories while reading along with the text. This can help promote fluency and increase comprehension skills.

When using taped books, a child should first listen to the tape of the story in its entirety without the book. Afterward, the child listens to the tape as he or she reads along with the text. This should be repeated as many times as necessary to gain fluency and decoding proficiency. Next, the child reads the story without help from the tape, referring to sections of the tape only when necessary. Any challenging words that they come across should be written down on a 3 × 5 index card with the word on one side and the sentence it appears in on the other side. These cards should be stored in a word box to be reviewed in later sessions. They can then read the story aloud when a parent is available or later on in the week. Children can make their own tape recording of the story as a form of positive reinforcement to gain greater confidence in fluency.

It is a good idea for parents and teachers to confer throughout the year concerning progress made at home. The more information a parent shares with the teacher, the better informed the teacher will be in planning lessons and activities, and he or she will be in a better position to plan remedial strategies and supportive supplementary interventions.

You can also keep track of progress made at home by using the record sheets below (see textboxes 8.3 and 8.4). Use the form shown in Table 8.1 at the end of every book shared and finished to record a child's progress.

Continuously track a child's progress at the culmination of every book. Share this information with your child and teacher and plan the next steps to be addressed during the next book. You can also help the student create his or her own self-evaluation record sheet to be used in conjunction with the formal one on the previous page to gauge how the student feels about the program. Bring these reports to the next parent-teacher conference.

TEXTBOX 8.3 MY PINPOINT READING RECORD

Activity Record Sheet
Title of Book: _____
Author: _____
Date Started: _____
Today's Date: _____
An interesting activity we did together: _____
Next steps for tomorrow: _____
_____
_____
_____
_____
_____

TEXTBOX 8.4 PINPOINT READING TIME SHEET

Book Title	Date Started	Date Finished
Week #1	Total Number of Pages Read	Weekly Points Earned
Monday:		
Tuesday:		
Wednesday		
Thursday:		
Friday:		
Saturday:		
Sunday:		

IDEA BANK

Familiarize yourself with the process and try to stick to the format. It may take several days and/or weeks to learn how to do this properly.

Practice with your child on a daily basis.

Table 8.1.

Name of Book		Date Finished	
Date Started			

Criteria:	Yes/No	Evidence	Next Steps
Oral Reading:			
Reads smoothly and evenly			
Uses expression and observes punctuation			
Self-corrects errors, substitutions, and omissions			
Rereads a sentence when it doesn't make sense			
Word Recognition:			
Uses sight vocabulary, phonics			
Uses context clues and structural clues to identify words			
Comprehension:			
Identifies major story elements			
Makes predictions			
Summarizes and integrates information			
Demonstrates prior knowledge; sets a purpose			
Reviews and rereads during reading			
Writing:			
Uses details in writing to communicate an effective message			
Uses correct punctuation and capitalization			
Uses correct spelling of words			
Expresses ideas clearly in writing			
General Items:			
Chooses to read during free time at home			
Enjoys and cooperates with the program			
Needs extra supportive help at school			

Chapter Nine

The Art of Questioning

The Pinpoint Reading program requires the parent or other helper to provide specific questions to bring out the essence of the meaning of every sentence in a paragraph. It helps children extend their thinking by asking them demanding, in-depth questions about their reading. The power lies in crafting questions that point to specific extraction of textual material and in the discussions about what the questions demand the reader to do.

After completing a passage of a paragraph or two, ask follow-up questions or prompts such as the following:

Why?
Prove that.
Do you agree?
How do you know?
Explain what you just said; I didn't understand it.
Tell me more.
Can you give me an example or another reason why?

When asking these questions, challenge the child to defend and support his or her conclusions and opinions against different points of view that you bring up. Ask the child to describe how he or she arrived at the answers. Try to bring out additional possible answers to the sole answer that may have been given. Finally, let the child generate some of his or her own questions.

Use these probing sample questions to clarify and elicit information and analysis about the various elements of a story:

Characterization:

What did you learn about the most important character in the story?
What did you learn about other characters in the story?
What does the main character do in the story?
What words does the author use to describe the character?
Why do you think the author used these words to describe the character?
Is this character real or imaginary? How do you know?
If you were this character, what would you do differently?
Which character did you like best?

Plot:

What is the main problem faced by the character?
When does the problem begin?
What do the characters do to try to solve the problem?
How is the problem solved?
What happens after the problem is solved?
Was there another way that you might have solved the problem?
Does the end of the story make sense? Is it logical, surprising, or confusing?

Setting:

How does the author describe where the story took place?
Did the story take place in the past, present, future, or a combination of times?
Does the description of the characters fit the place that the action is said to have occurred?
Does the description of the characters fit the time that the action is said to have occurred?

Mood:

How did the story make you feel?
What did the author do to make you feel this way?

Theme:

What is the main point or idea of the story?
Are there ideas in the story you can relate to?
What does the story tell you about people?
What does the story tell you about the world?

Style/Genre:

What type of story is this?
Who is telling the story? How do you know?
Is it being told in the first or third person?

Language:

What did the author mean by this sentence, word, or phrase?
What does the word _____ make you think of?
How does the word _____ make you feel?
Explain the meaning of this simile/metaphor.
Why did the author compare _____ to _____?
What other types of figurative language did the author use?

General:

At what point in the story did you like the main character the most or the least?
Did the ending surprise you? Why or why not?
What were the hints the author gave you about how the story would end?
If you were to rewrite the story for a different time period, when would it be? Why? How would you change the story?
If you were to put yourself in the story, what character would you be most like? Why?
Describe the main conflict of the story. How was it resolved?

Ask children to write a critique or short summary for the book just finished by addressing these points:

Who was in the book? What did they do?
Where did they do it?
When did they do it?
Why did they do it?
Why did you or did you not like this book?
How would you rate this book on a scale of 1–10?
How would your parents rate this book on a scale of 1–10?

Questioning helps give children a purpose for reading. Sometimes it is just as crucial to get a child to generate his or her own questions, and encourage and enable them to do so, as it is to ask questions of the child. These questions should focus on the things that interest a child about the topic or theme; they may or may not be questions that are exactly relevant to the story.

Try to help children develop questions that require a variety of thought processes. For example, help them ask questions that require retrieving basic knowledge or that ask for interpretation or explanation. Have them apply what they have learned from the text by asking questions that solve, illustrate, or classify; questions that analyze what has been learned; synthesis-type questions that ask a child to predict or plan; and evaluative questions that ask a child to judge or decide.

But as you attempt to construct the right questions, always try to get the child to give alternative responses. Tell the child that there may not necessarily be just one correct answer. Encourage the child to think.

One way to enhance comprehension through questioning is to keep a "Question Box" with accompanying activities. Write these questions on index cards, place them in a coffee can or shoebox, and have a child choose one per day according to the story he or she is reading:

1. At what point in the story did you admire the main character the most? Who did you admire the least? Why?
2. Did your story have a surprise ending? Why or why not?
3. What clues did the author give you about how the story would end?

4. If you were the author and wanted to change the ending, how would you do it and why?
5. Change the actions of a character in the story and give that character a new identity.
6. How would you act if you were the main character in the story? What would you do differently?
7. Write a short song, poem, or rhyme based on the story.
8. Was the vocabulary in the book you just read easy, average, or hard? Identify one new word, find the definition, and write a sentence for it.
9. Identify the main problem in the story. How was it solved?
10. Would you recommend this book to a friend? Tell why or why not.

Competent readers always question what they are reading while they are reading. You want to help children ask questions before, during, and after reading that will serve to advance the skill of comprehension by making the meaning of reading passages clearer.

Such questions help children make cogent predictions about what will happen next in a story, figure out the author's purpose, and find the right answer on a test. In some cases, standardized test reading passages are not as hard to decipher as the complex questions often asked of the student regarding those passages.

Encourage children to use sticky notes to place near the text itself for recording a question as it comes up. Ask them to stop at places in the text that trigger questions in their minds and write them down on the notes. They can further discuss the questions with a partner before attempting to answer them. As they continue to read the passage, they can refer back to the sticky note to serve as a reminder about what answer they are searching for.

Another method of questioning is using the Socratic Seminar approach. Socrates once said: "The only true wisdom is in knowing you know nothing." We can't assume that children know what we think they know. The Socratic method of teaching is based on Socrates' theory that it is more important to enable students to think for themselves than to provide them with the "right" answer.

Socrates engaged his students in dialogue by responding to their questions with questions. This process allows students to explore topics in a way that allows them to express their own ideas and interpretations.

Socratic questioning recognizes that questions, not answers, are the driving force in thinking. Socratic seminars explore ideas, values, and issues drawn from readings chosen for their richness and depth.

Socratic Seminars can help children:

1. Learn through critical thought.
2. Engage in meaningful class or at home discussions.
3. Create a cooperative learning environment where students are allowed to bring various points of view to the discussion.
4. Develop meaningful dialogue in addition to discussion and debate. Dialogue is different in that it allows for a free and open exchange of ideas without bias or prejudice.
5. Develop divergent thinking rather than only convergent.
6. Foster new ideas and mutual respect as all ideas are listened to without interruption.

There are nine steps that teachers and parents can use for developing a Socratic Seminar: Children are prepared by having read the assignment, book, or story, etc.

1. Children form a circle.
2. The teacher or parent presents opening questions.
3. Children respond to each other.
4. The teacher or parent probes or clarifies only non-judgmentally.
5. The teacher asks some questions.
6. The students respond to each other.
7. The teacher/parent presents closing questions.
8. Children personalize discussion.
9. Hold an evaluative debriefing post-session.

Here are a few more tips:

A. When using Socratic Seminars, it is important that the facilitator (teacher or parent) assigns a text before the class or at home. The text can be a portion of a novel, a poem, news article, on-line feature, essay, or short story.

B. It is important to ask the children one of the following types of questions:

1. A World Connection question: Write a question connecting the text to the real world.

2. A Close-Ended question: Write a question about the text that will help everyone in the class come to an agreement on characters or plot points in the text. There is usually a "right" answer here.

3. An Open-Ended question: Write a question that will require insight, proof, group discussion, and logic in order to explore various ways to answer the question.

4. A Universal Theme/Core question: Write a question that deals with themes of a text that will encourage group discussion about the universality of the story.

5. A Literary Analysis question: Write a question dealing with HOW the author chose to compose a literary piece which can include but is not limited to the author's point of view, characters, archetypical hero, patterns, poetic form, etc.

IDEA BANK

The important thing to remember at every juncture in the reading is to ask penetrating and specific questions geared to get your child to think and think again about the reading material being analyzed.

Chapter Ten

Pairing and Sharing

For the wine enthusiast and foodies out there, striving to enhance meals with pairing a good wine with good food is absolutely axiomatic. Teachers and parents can do the same, except instead of food we substitute good teacher ideas with good parent activities. Here are some good activities for both teachers and parents:

Teacher: Read all genres of literature but balance fiction with non-fiction books.

Parent: Make sure there is an ample supply of differentiated books that can comprise a read-aloud home library as well as books your child can read independently.

Teacher: Teach the organization and structure of fiction and non-fiction books.

Parent: Read more informational books at home and have them take them wherever you go. Use your car's back seat mesh accessory holders which usually face your children and fill them with a few books.

Teacher: Read more books of a practical "how-to" nature such as cooking, building projects, or saving money in a bank, making change and calculating sales tax, etc. Have some "make-it" and "take-it" fun activity projects involving reading and writing.

Parent: Read-aloud books that encourage children to explore new horizons such as building a wooden birdhouse, playing a musical instrument, how to paint, draw, sketch, watercolor, etc.

Teacher: Read more books on science, history, especially earth science and weather.

Parent: Read to your child about the unusual weather events occurring in the United States and around the globe. Challenge your child to find out why our weather has become more unusual or violent, using Internet searches.

Teacher: Have children read major documents from famous people such as the personal letters of Abraham Lincoln or the actual Declaration of Independence or the Emancipation Proclamation, etc.

Parent: Find naturalization papers, old passports, birth certificates, old letters, and postcards and share them with your child. Try to get your child interested in stamp or coin collection as they are wonderful avenues at learning history, culture, and geography.

Teacher: Find and discuss controversial books that explode the myths surrounding our culture, history, or scientific beliefs.

Parent: For example, parents can find books or articles that debunk the concept of global warming or that possibly recycling paper, for instance, is not cost effective or that green cars do nothing to help the environment or who among our past presidents did irreverent things. Did George Washington really cut down a cherry tree? Get kids to think critically.

Teacher: Teachers must constantly find ways to allow students to prove what they have uncovered in literature.

Parent: Parents can ask to uncover key clues and evidence as they allow their children to become literacy detectives.

Teacher: Teachers must find ways to help children arrive at and uncover an author's point of view. Can authors be biased about certain topics they write about?

Parent: Parents can help kids compare and contrast various titles by the same author to uncover similar features, or to see how the author treats subjects differently using dissimilar techniques.

Teacher: Help students own new vocabulary so they can fix them in their minds and use them in their written work. Study roots, word clusters, prefixes, suffixes, multiple meaning words, and word families.

Parent: Fix words in your child's mind by having them hear-see-say them and then having them place the word or phrase in context using creative, descriptive sentences that illuminates the meaning or what we call meaningful sentences

Teacher: Model good teaching by using higher order vocabulary that is challenging and thought provoking. Also have your students see you read at your desk.

Parent: Encourage your child by setting a good example. Read after dinner. Let your child see you read. Show them that reading is relaxing, enjoyable, calming, educational, and just plain fun. Limit electronic games and TV.

Teachers use word walls to facilitate word identification and word knowledge, parents can utilize that same technique at home using this "Wallpaper" strategy:

Place the difficult, hard to understand word or phrase on a chart. Define it, put it in a sentence, use it in a different context and show variations. Hang this chart on a wall in your home in several different places by making copies, including the bathrooms, hallways, etc.

Remove and add new charts when necessary. Try to keep the old charts up in different locations or in a portfolio where they can be easily retrieved.

Make these wallpaper charts interactive with your child by having him or her sign the chart showing that they have read and understood the word or phrase and dating it next to their signature. Students can also indicate that they still "don't get it."

If they are having trouble with a certain paragraph or page in a story, parents can encapsulate the passage by writing a paragraph interpretation chart using the author's words mixed in with your own words to help facilitate comprehension. It is as if you are remixing parts of the story so they can be easily digested by your child. This is similar to the technique we refer to as paraphrasing.

Children can create their own charts entitled: "I need customer assistance!" They then enter the words or phrases they are still having trouble with.

Teachers can have a section of their classroom depicting a "Drive-Thru Menu."

Students tell the teacher what they need, or what the problem is by writing their request in an "Order Here" box. Next to that box is another box entitled "Pick Up Your Answer Here" where the teacher can write in a possible solution. Parents can do this at home as well.

IDEA BANK

Do not forget to expose your child to a wide variety of literature as well as making sure they are supplied with those specific topics they have interest in.

Chapter Eleven

Note Taking

You get a phone call from Mom and she asks you to take the meat out of the freezer so it can defrost in time for supper's roast, take out the garbage, close the window in the bedroom because it's raining, and feed the kitties. While you're wearing your headset with that rock song screaming in your ear, there is a lot of information to remember. So instead of memorizing everything, you quickly grope for a piece of paper from the memo pad hanging on the wall and write down everything (or pretty much everything) that you heard.

Writing down short ideas, reminders, or important facts while reading them or listening is called taking notes. If your child is concerned that note taking might be too difficult, use your own version of the above story as a reminder that he or she probably already takes notes all the time, perhaps without realizing it. Notes help a student remember ideas while reading a long paragraph so that when the student gets to the last sentence, he or she will not have forgotten much of the important stuff. On tests, note taking may be required, so it is an important skill to learn.

Here are some note-taking hints:

1. Jot a note every time an important event is mentioned.
2. Jot a note about someone doing something important or saying something special.
3. Jot down any other important details that tell what the story will be about.
4. Use short jottings—only a few words. There is no need to write in complete sentences.

Students can use the graphic organizer shown below to help take good notes when reading all types of material, especially informational books. This will help guide them through the maze of facts and concepts encountered on test-reading material, especially more difficult material such as science or social studies/history passages.

TEXTBOX 11.1 MY NOTE PAD

TOPIC	MAIN IDEA	JOTTINGS
List topic	Identify main idea	List details

Or use a semantic word map like the one below:

TEXTBOX 11.2 TOPIC: PARAKEETS

What They Do	Where Are They From?	Looks Like?
eat seeds	Australia	multicolored

Or use the semantic web by including the focal question or the statement that the test requires you to delve into:

TEXTBOX 11.3
WHY DO PARAKEETS MAKE GOOD PETS?

Sings and chirps	Cheap to buy	Low maintenance

When reading fictional material, students could use the note-taking format shown in textbox 11.4.

Sticky notes work very well and can be placed directly inside the text for instant review. Taking notes on 3 × 5 index cards is another alternative; these can be alphabetized or categorized according to subject for quick reference and placed in card files for safekeeping. A sample sticky note or card is shown in textbox 11.4.

TEXTBOX 11.4 NOTE-TAKING FORMAT FOR FICTIONAL MATERIAL

List: Title/Topic: _____

Subtitles/Topic: _____

Objectives: _____

Theme: _____

Main Idea: _____

Unusual Vocabulary: _____

Record predictions: _____

Record questions about what might happen: _____

Record author's purpose: _____

Record critical points: _____

Additional notes to take after reading:
I found the important items I was looking for. They are: _____
_____.

I'm not sure I understand _____.

This story was mainly about_____.

Draw conclusions based on evidence:
The author's purpose was to_____.

The main characters turned out to be _____.

The most interesting part for me was _____.

Some reading standardized tests call upon the student to take notes during the listening comprehension section. In this part, the students will have to listen to a story read aloud by the teacher without the benefit of having the text in front of them to review. They listen to the story twice. The first time they hear the story, they will be asked to just listen carefully. As they listen to the story a second time, they are allowed to take notes. The notes will be used to answer questions, but the notes themselves do not count

TEXTBOX 11.5 STICKY NOTE/INDEX CARD FORMAT

Topic:
 Who:
 What:
 When:
 Where:
 Why:
 How:
Other key information:

toward a final score. Students may use their notes to complete a graphic organizer based on the plot of the story or the sequence of events.

Next, they may be asked to use their notes to write a summary or to draw conclusions based on the outcome of the story. The last task would be to write a composition about some facet of the story.

The composition will be marked on how clearly the student organizes and expresses ideas, how accurately and completely the student answers the questions, how well the student supports ideas with examples, how interesting and enjoyable the writing is, how correctly a student uses grammar, spelling, and punctuation, and how well the student organizes paragraphs.

IDEA BANK

In addition to reinforcing what note taking is, note taking can be accomplished on-line making it simpler to collect and organize research material for their assignments and projects. It is relatively easy and quickly accessible. One tool is Yahoo! Note Pad at www.yahoo.com. This also makes it possible to share their information and ideas with their teachers and peers.

Chapter Twelve

Probing

In an informal way, teach children to constantly probe for information and new vocabulary or even old vocabulary that they can decode but do not understand. For instance, they may read the word *however*, but do they know what that word signals within the text? When they read the word *this*, do they know what *this* refers to in the text? It was always easy to teach a second-grader how to pronounce the word *atom*. It was just very hard to try to teach him or her what that word meant.

Probing really means questioning everything that is relevant within the material being read. Children should learn to make reading "pit stops" to question and think at least once in a given section or paragraph.

Read to a point. If a child is having trouble with the words or with understanding, probe the hot spots by reading and reviewing an unusual word, phrase, expression, or idea at least a second or third time.

Stop and go back if something does not make sense or sound right; then go back and clarify, confirm, or identify further problematic words or understandings. Ask, "Does that make sense? Do you understand what you're reading?" You could use sticky notes as next-day reminders to review materials from the previous day. Try to agree or disagree with, like or not like, and question the author's purpose.

Probing should be done where and when necessary, instead of just focusing on one page, one paragraph, or even one sentence that has children mindlessly read through a book, page after page, without challenging them as they read. It isn't the quantity but the quality of the experience. Reading aloud is just not enough. We have to take it up a notch. We have to challenge and inspire our children to dissect whatever reading material they are perusing. Try to make this a part of the daily routine, but do not make it onerous or too repetitive. Pick and choose where a child should stop to probe the material at hand.

For probing specific parts of the reading material, choose any or all of the following strategies:

1. Find several parts of the story that show how a character changes his attitude or way of behaving.
2. Find sentences or paragraphs that show traits of the character, humorous passages, sad or tragic events, vivid or picturesque descriptions, or imagery used by the author.
3. Find the ending of the story and be ready to predict what would likely happen after the story is over.
4. Find the part of the story that you feel shows cause for something that happened later in the story.
5. Find a part of the story you think could not really have happened.
6. Find specific traits of two characters in the story and compare and contrast them using the Venn diagram located in the appendix.
7. Locate the main idea or theme of the story.
8. Find a part of the story that reveals facts you never knew before.
9. Find a part of the story that proves a personal opinion you believe in.
10. Locate the part of the rising action and the climax.
11. Find an unusual or interesting conversation between two characters.
12. Locate a part of the story that tells how something was created or made, how something happened, how a sport is played, or how a craft is constructed.
13. Search for phrases that paint vivid pictures of people, places, situations, settings, or actions.

When probing for certain specific aspects of a passage, it may be helpful for students to talk to themselves as they read the text about what they are trying to look for. Table 12.1 has a chart of critical reading strategies. Show students how to use it by modeling a few of them.

Probing helps the reader dig deeper into the hidden meaning of text. It helps one read between the lines to unlock the nuances of language and get underneath the author's message. Tests seek to challenge students to think, not just to know. A child should learn to read test questions as critically as the test passages themselves.

Probing to find the best answer to comprehension questions is a critical skill. A student should read the selection completely before beginning to answer the question. The student should think about a possible answer first, then look for it in the answer choices. The student should then read all the choices before making a selection, then go back to the reading passage and skim and scan to locate the correct answer or information. The student should ask him- or herself the following questions:

Which is the best answer to the question?
Why is this the best answer?
Which words or phrases gave the best clues or the most information?
Where does the story say it? Tell why.
Can I explain this answer?
I'm not sure about this answer; I'm going back for one more try.

Before committing to an answer, students should attempt to classify the question based on one of the following considerations. These considerations may suggest a particular strategy to follow:

1. The answer might be located right there on the page within the test paragraph. If so, the words used to make up the question and the words used to answer the question are right there in the same sentence.
2. If the answer is not directly found, think and search for the answer by connecting ideas from different parts of the test paragraph as you read. Words for the question and words for the answer may not be found directly in the same sentence, but come from different places in the text.
3. The answer may not be in the story at all; however, the author has given information that can be put together with what is already known. The person constructing the test assumes the student has some prior knowledge to answer the question.
4. There is the possibility that students must answer the question all by themselves. In this case, they need to think about what they already know through prior learning or experiences with the subject matter. In these cases, the answer can be arrived at without even reading the selection.

Table 12.1. Critical Reading Strategies

Talking to Myself (Mouth Closed)

Probing Objective	What Should I Say?
Main Idea/Supportive Details	I'm supposed to find the main idea in this story. The title is _____ so it is probably about _____. I'll keep reading and try to find some details to help me understand the main idea. Some of the details that I found were _____, _____, and _____, so I guess the main idea is _____.
Cause/Effect	I'm not sure what caused this event to happen. If I go back to the action in the story, I can recall that _____ and _____ happened earlier. So I think that _____ was caused by _____.
Drawing Conclusions	What am I feeling about this topic? The author said that _____, _____, and _____ happened. How does that relate to what I already know about what has happened so far? Did this ever happen to my friends or me? What really happened in the story? Based on what I have read, I think that _____.
Compare/Contrast	Why are _____ and _____ alike and how are they different? I think I should review the story to see if _____ and _____ were both _____. But I know that one did _____ and the other did _____. If I compare and contrast _____ and _____, I can see that _____.
Fantasy/Reality	I'm not sure if I can tell the difference between what is fact and what is fiction. The people in this story look like and talk like normal human beings, but they landed on Earth in flying saucers from the planet Zoodik. This story must be a fantasy or science fiction because these things do not happen in real life.
Fact/Opinion	I'm not sure if I understand what is a fact and what is an opinion. The main character uses words like hate and dislike. I know that these words are more of a personal feeling type. The sentence must be the character's opinion.
Author's Purpose	Why did the author write this story? If I think about what I have already read, I can see that the writer is trying to convince me to think about _____. It must be that the author's purpose is to _____.

Students who are encouraged to think about the questions and the source of the answers to a reading passage, and who are given sufficient practice, increase their competence at finding the correct answer to a given question by building their sensitivity to the various kinds of questions and sources of information that they encounter.

Another strategy that students can use as they try to discern an answer is to cross out the obviously wrong answers, thereby using the process of elimination to pare down the choices. Usually tests will not penalize students for incorrect answers. It is therefore better to try to guess at unknown answers than to leave them blank.

Time is also another factor. Children should budget their time. They should work as quickly and efficiently as possible without wasting undue time on a single question, especially if the question is extremely hard. They can keep on going and return to the difficult question if they have time remaining.

Children should also be given practice in filling in the complete answer space and in erasing a mark or stray mark completely when they do change an answer. The electronic marking process may read an erroneously marked answer and choose the wrong answer. It is critical to remind children of the need for entering each answer in its proper position on the answer grid.

In addition, demonstrate how one misplaced answer will affect the placement and scoring of all subsequent answers, which can lead to a domino effect of unwitting and unheeded continuous error. This usually occurs after a child skips an answer due to difficulty or switches to another column of answers and does not stay dedicated to the continuous order of the test answer grid.

IDEA BANK

Allow no stone unturned when it comes to details in the story being read. Question everything. Assume nothing. Encourage your child to ask questions about content they do not understand or words that are confusing.

Chapter Thirteen

Phonics

Phonics is the knowledge of letter/sound relationships and how they are used in reading and spelling. The primary goal of phonics instruction is to help beginning readers understand how letters are linked to sounds to form letter-sound connections and to help them learn how to apply this knowledge in their reading.

Usually if a child hasn't mastered work attack with intensive and well-applied systematic phonics instruction by third grade, they most likely would not benefit from further intensive phonics instruction. Phonics instruction is most effective in the lower grades, where it is usually completed by the end of the first grade.

When working with upper-grade elementary students, you can usually incorporate a program of incidental phonics instruction which does not follow a planned, systematic format of phonics skills to guide instruction, but instead highlights specific elements when they appear in the text.

You can assist children by making a set of phonics cards for only those sounds they are having trouble with. On one side of the card, print the letter. On the other side of the card, make a list of words containing that sound, including the troublesome word. Try to elicit some of the words from the student.

For example, let's say the student is having trouble with the "ch" sound. Review the cards using the following steps:

1. Have the student hear the sound of "ch" in the words on the back of the card by reviewing the list of "ch" words (just listening, not looking at the words).

2. Review the list of "ch" words on the card, accentuating the "ch" sound as the student sees each word but does not say them yet.
3. Say the first "ch" word on the card and have the child repeat it.
4. Say the word again.
5. Have the student repeat it.
6. Repeat this process for each "ch" word on the card.
7. Make the "ch" sound again.
8. Ask the child for the "ch" sound by prompting this way: What letters make the sound of "ch"?
9. What sound does the letters "ch" make?
10. Ask the student to create a sentence using one of the "ch" words on the card such as making a tongue twister: "How much wood should a woodchuck chuck if the woodchuck could chuck wood?"

You could purchase some commercially-made phonics games in a teacher bookstore, mall bookstore, or online. Or you can create your own phonics games and activities such as the one called *WORDO*.

Let's say you are reviewing the "short a" sound, as in the word *bat*. Make a bingo-type word game card looking something like textbox 13.1. You can call out only words with the "short a" sound, or you can call out all words. Show each word on a card as you say it. Or say that you are thinking of a word that rhymes with *ham*. A child wins when he or she gets *WORDO* of *all* words correctly identified with the "short a" sound. Check that all the words are correct by having the child say each one aloud while pointing to the word.

If, for instance, someone has trouble saying the word *smart*, try to break it down by teaching the "sm" sound first. Ask for a list of words beginning with "sm" and make a list. Then review the list by first saying the word and then having the students repeat. Just point to the word and wait for them to repeat. Also block out the word with a piece of paper and ask them to say the word from memory. Then ask for "art" words and have the students make another list. It would be helpful to make word ladders such as *art—cart—carting—carter*. Help students create rhymes with "art" words, for example, "The dog chased me in the park, and when it got mad, it started to bark."

You can also help students identify word endings, prefixes, suffixes, root words, and compound words. Try a variety of techniques. But before

TEXTBOX 13.1 SAMPLE WORDO CARD

W	O	R	D	O
bit	bat	bet	boat	ban
cat	rat	fat	hat	land
mat	jam	tin	sun	sat
bin	pat	tan	ball	bat
had	old	fan	can	light

you tell them an unknown word, ask them to sound it out, keep reading until they unlock the word through context clues (i.e., reading information right before and right after the suspect word), ask them to think about the word, and use any pictures that might offer clues.

If all else fails, tell them the word. Repeat and review the words several times to make sure they are learned and retained in their memory.

You can also help a child decode words by breaking them apart by the syllables (or "chunks") in the word. Tackling multisyllabic words can be arduous and challenging. For example, with the word *immediately*, you could show a child how to clap it out to find the different syllables. Teach them to find chunks. On a chart, place the word and draw a line or use different colored magic markers to separate out each chunk. Break it down thus:

Im—me—di—ate—ly

Sometimes just getting the first two or three chunks will start the process of identifying the word because of the child's prior experience and knowledge. Oftentimes I have just gotten through the *im—me—di* parts and the children, after hearing the word elsewhere, now are able to place all the pieces of the puzzle together. You could use the chart in Textbox 13.2 to help them unlock difficult words. Use some sample words and model the use of the chart.

When a child asks for help with word recognition, first give them a few moments to figure it out by themselves. They can reread the sentence that contains the tough word. Just tell them to try the word again. Asking questions like "Does that make sense?" causes the child to think about

TEXTBOX 13.2 WORD "UNLOCKING" CHART

What Strategy Did I Use to Figure Out a Word Today?
I went back and reread.
I used the pictures from the book.
I tried to sound it out.
I skipped it and kept reading.
I kept thinking about the word.
I finally asked for help.

meaning, or "Does it look right to you and sound right?" focuses on the structure of the word.

But as a rule of thumb, the older your child gets, the best way to have them learn new words, after going through the above procedures, is to tell them the word and then have them repeat the word and the sentence that contains the word at least twice.

IDEA BANK

Phonics can be a useful tool in word identification. Keep in mind that when all else fails, repeated holistic scrutiny of the troublesome word, just saying the word over and over again and discussing the meaning as well, is a worthwhile tactic.

Chapter Fourteen

The Strategic Reader

Students should be able to think more about the process of reading than merely reading the printed word and understanding it. They should monitor their own comprehension by keeping pace with the information being read. Many times they just read word by word and are not thinking about the text. They process nothing. Keeping pace with their reading involves:

1. Knowing that comprehension is occurring—monitoring.
2. Knowing what is being comprehended.
3. Knowing how to repair or fix comprehension—regulating.

Students should be asking themselves as they read:

1. Do I understand what I'm reading?
2. Does this sentence or paragraph make sense?
3. Do I need to go back and reread?

Use the chart in textbox 14.1 to help them self-monitor.

Before a child reads anything, ask for a prediction of what might happen in the story or what might happen next. When they finish reading, ask them to retell or summarize what was just read. Do this in short sections. Don't let them read several pages ahead before checking comprehension. Summarizing is an effective postreading technique that research shows fosters increased understanding and remembering. Students must learn to do summaries when called for on standardized tests; this can be taught by having them state the topic being summarized and telling what action or

TEXTBOX 14.1 SELF-MONITORING CHECKLIST

Before reading:
    What is my purpose for reading?
    What do I already know?
    Why do I need to know more?
    What can I predict?
    Is this similar to anything I have ever read before?
    What am I going to get out of this book?

During reading:
    Does what I am reading make sense to me?
    I will reread this passage to make sure I understand it.
    What can I do if I am confused?
    What new information am I learning about?
    Can I use this new learning somewhere else?
    What do I still need to learn?
    Is this stuff interesting or enjoyable to me? Why or why not?

After reading:
    I will summarize the chapter in my own words.
    Where can I go to learn some more ideas?
    I will then ask myself:
        What did I learn?
        How can I use the things I learned today?
        What parts of the story did I like, or didn't I like, and why?
    Do I still have some unanswered questions from the story?

events happen in the beginning, middle, and end. Using a plot organization chart like the one in textbox 14.2 can help students organize those critical sections of the story and develop, from the sum of those parts, a cogent summary.

Also, it's a good idea to review all of the elements in a story after the story is read. I usually ask students to fill out a story map like the one in textbox 14.3.

TEXTBOX 14.2 PLOT/RELATIONSHIP CHART

Somebody	*Wanted*	*But*	*So*
Characters	Goals/Motivation	Conflict	Resolution

Summary:

_____

_____

_____

_____

A simple retelling of the story or sections of the story can also strengthen comprehension. In a simple retelling, the student can first discuss, then re-write the story (or a section of it) in a five-to-seven event sequence. Each event is then illustrated and matched to the appropriate text.

An additional activity is known as Reader's Theater. It is actually a form of acting out a story without really acting. After selecting a story, followed by a retelling and discussion, prepare a script based on the dialogue taken from the story. Ask children to read specifically chosen speaking parts of the characters. Other students could act as narrators, reading the nonspeaking parts. You can interchange narration and dia-logue parts. Rehearse this as you would a play. Use facial expressions, gestures, inflections, and sound effects. Practice your fluency. Reread parts until fluency is satisfactory. But above all else, have fun with it.

To help strategic readers increase their comprehension power, stopping points should be used to assess what is being read. Stopping points should come frequently in the middle of a passage, at the end of a passage, or after a paragraph or two, depending upon the difficulty of the material. During the reading, ask pointed questions that require them to stop and check for answers. Ask them to skim and scan to locate vital information.

TEXTBOX 14.3 STORY MAP

Story Title:
Author:
The Setting:
  Main Characters:
  Place (include multiple places and settings):
  Time (indicate past, present, or future):
The Problem:
The Goal:
Sequence of Events:
  Event 1:
  Event 2:
  Event 3:
  Event 4:
  Event 5:
  Event 6:
The Resolution or Solution:

Ask plenty of *why* questions and fewer of *who* or *what*. Ask questions that can evoke thoughtful responses.

Get the students to think. Get students to think about thinking about reading. Ask your child to develop his or her own set of questions to ask you. Instead of the more basic types of *who* or *what* questions, ask questions to help them focus on analysis and interpretation that will help them really read between the lines, for example:

Do you know of another instance where someone was harmed like the main character was?
What event in the story could not have happened?
What would be a possible solution to his problem?
Defend your position about the main character's actions.

Ask probing, thoughtful questions that lead to a student's "unpacking" their thinking as they slice through information:

TEXTBOX 14.4 MONITORING MY UNDERSTANDING

What Did You Do When You Came Across a Passage, Phrase, or Sentence That You Didn't Understand?
Mark which of the following strategies you used:
Reread
Stopped and thought about it
Asked questions
Kept reading
Wrote about it
Asked someone

"Tell me more."
"How did you come to thinking this way?" "Prove it."
"Where does it say that in the story?"

We can't assume that students know everything, or that they know what we know about a passage just because they've read it well. They may be fine word readers but may lack a capacity for understanding new ideas and facts. It may make perfect sense to you, but not to a student. Another chart students can use to aid in their understanding of difficult passages is given in textbox 14.4.

Children need to forensically explore and dissect our language. They need to see the structures, our language patterns, the meanings and understandings of the printed word, and the author's purpose in writing what they wrote. Leave no word, phrase, or expression untouched. Wring out every possible nuance, thought, and concept until the printed message is clearly understood.

IDEA BANK

The idea of children tracking their own progress as they read by constantly attempting to gain meaning from the text is a critical skill that should be taught at home and in school and should be constantly reinforced.

Chapter Fifteen

Writing

Some standardized tests ask students to write in response to literature. Those portions of the test are often graded using a skills rubric and are marked holistically by at least two teacher reviewer/evaluators who must reach a consensus about a child's written work using the rubric as their guide. How fair is this? Can these reviewers remain objective? Are they well trained to perform this task? Are sharp disagreements adjudicated in a fair manner so consensus is reached?

The only way to assure that a student responds appropriately to the question is to make sure they completely and carefully respond to the question. Students should follow these guidelines when being asked on a test to complete a written response:

1. Read the question carefully.
2. If there is a planning page, use it by taking notes and writing a short outline.
3. After the planning page is filled out, begin to write a response by turning the question around and using it as a topic sentence to start the answer.
4. If there are several bulleted points that require students to respond, then have them check off each point that they have covered in their writing as they are done.
5. Make sure they write complete sentences with correct spelling, punctuation, and grammar.

6. The teacher/evaluators may rely on a writing rubric based on a student's grade level (see table 15.1). The numerical value shows a hierarchy of evaluation whereby a 1 would be the lowest mark with a 4 being the highest mark. Usually a 1 or 2 are unsatisfactory marks and a 3 or 4 are acceptable marks. Corresponding criteria are listed below each number. Written subskills being assessed are listed on the right. They may also benefit from this self-tune-up editing checklist:

7. Have I read my writing aloud? Does it sound right?

8. Is there any part that doesn't sound right?

9. Do all my sentences make sense?

10. Is my writing organized in the best possible way?

11. Do all my sentences have an ending mark?

12. Have I used quotation marks, commas, and parentheses correctly?

13. Have I used capitals for all proper nouns and at the beginning of each new sentence?

14. Have I checked for misspelled words? Have I worked on them?

15. In addition, you can motivate, encourage, and monitor a child's writing by developing a literature log. Literature logs can help them make meaningful connections to the written material. They can help facilitate comprehension and expand students' knowledge and awareness. They can serve to help students organize and think about the meaning behind the writing material as well as to write more clearly and specifically. Every evening, the first and last part of the Pinpoint Reading process is having a child make an entry into a literature log, notebook, or journal.

The following are suggestions about what kinds of items to include in a literature log:

1. Personal Responses—writing personal reactions: I enjoyed ___. or I felt ___.

2. Descriptive Responses—recalling parts of a story such as plot, setting, or characters: Bob decides to ___. The story takes place in ___.

3. Interpretive Responses—hypothesizing about meaning: I think Joe is hiding his real feelings because ___. I think the author is saying that because ___.

4. Evaluative Responses—valuing and evaluating: I found the book very troublesome because ___. I think the author's message is very crucial because ___.

Table 15.1. Sample Writing Rubric

	4	3	2	1
Engagement	Great opening; reader wants to keep reading	Good opening; reader wants to keep reading	Has an opening; some parts are interesting	No opening; uninteresting
Organization	Clearly organized; easy to understand	Somewhat organized but still understandable	Somewhat disorganized	Disorganized and confusing
Clarity	Stays on target with details that help reader's understanding	Includes a few details that help reader's understanding	Includes some details that do not make sense	Includes many details that don't make sense
Development	Everything pulls together; reader knows piece is finished without seeing "The End"	Reader is pretty sure piece is ready to end	Reader has an idea the piece is ending	Reader is surprised the piece is over
Sequence	Has a beginning, middle, and end; uses transitional words	Has a beginning, middle, and end	Missing beginning, middle, or end	No clear beginning, middle, or end
Mechanics	One or no errors in grammar, punctuation, or spelling	Makes a few errors	Many errors but still readable	Unreadable because of errors
Engagement Narrative	Used enough written description and specific details so that the reader can clearly see characters, setting, and problem	Used enough written description and specific details so that the reader can see the characters, setting, and problem	Reader has some idea of setting and characters	Reader has no idea about the setting and characters
Characterization	Reader knows characters well and can predict their actions	Reader knows characters	Reader has some idea what the characters are like	Reader has no idea of what the characters are like
Nonfiction report	Introduces, describes, and defines the topic in depth with very accurate details	Introduces and defines topic in some depth with several accurate details	Introduces the topic with one or two details but with some inaccuracies	Strays to other topics with no details
Reflecting Opinions	Has an opinion and convinces reader that it is reasonable	Has an opinion that is minimally supported	Has an opinion that is unsupported	Retells the story without stating opinion

In addition, students can create a double entry log. They make notes on the content of what they are reading in the left-hand column. These notes are factual and may include paraphrasing of text, quotations, references, lists, or examples. Students then can write personal responses in the right-hand column. These may include opinions, interpretations, comparisons, reflections, and analogies to their own life situations. Students can relate the new reading to other readings, provide agreements or disagreements with the statements, and jot down questions, new ideas, or vocabulary.

In literature logs, students can add small drawings and sketches to enhance their entries. In addition, if students have literature logs, there may not be a need to have a separate vocabulary book. If they come across words in the story that they want to learn to pronounce, use correctly, and understand, they can list these words on a vocabulary sheet or in the log with accompanying page numbers. Then they can look the words up in the dictionary.

Students can write a summary of all or part of the story and tell why they decided to summarize that particular part. In addition, when they find a special part in the book that they really like, they can write down the page number so they can remember where to find it and then write a few sentences about why they think it is special.

Also, students can create a list of questions based on how they feel about the story or about a certain part that needs clarification and greater understanding, or write about feelings and why the book makes them feel that way. They can talk about how the characters are feeling and acting. They can make predictions by writing down what they think might happen in the story, the next chapter, or the ending.

Determining the sequence of events in a story is another useful skill to help students understand the order of action and behavior of the main characters. Students can make a sequence chart, map, timeline, or list of events and tell why they think they are important.

Sometimes authors use special words, paint pictures, create mind movies, use humor, or use figurative language. Students can give examples of these items to show how the author attempts to make a story enjoyable. They could critique the author's work and write about things the author did well and things that the author could do better.

Students can learn to compare and contrast details in a story by telling how two things are alike or different; for example, they can analyze main characters that share similarities and differences. Sometimes what children are reading makes them think about another book they have read of the same genre. They can write what parts of the previously read book remind them of events in the current book and why they chose to write on those issues.

In addition, students can stop at some point during the story being read, pull out all of the new words they have written down so far, and use them to retell and record what they know about the story. They can also predict what will happen next in the story and how the story might end.

An activity called *story expressions* combines reading and writing and develops a child's ability to predict, activate, and focus on prior knowledge, and encourages higher-level thinking rather than asking only basic questions. Choose about ten to fifteen words or phrases from the story that outline the main points of the story, and ask for the student to predict what the story will be about and how the main points are connected. Or you can choose words from each chapter in larger books to introduce the main points of that chapter.

An additional activity is to, once again, stop the reading at certain points and have the student summarize what has happened using one or two sentences. Then have the student sketch what he or she thinks will happen next. Continue with the reading and repeat this strategy, comparing the sketch to what actually happens in the story. This idea can be incorporated when using chapter books; students can summarize the end of a chapter and then draw their predictions for the next chapter.

After finishing the entire book, students can do some of the following activities that will strengthen their understanding of the stories and application of information learned:

- *Summary:* For fiction, discuss the major issues of the plot and make a list of the key points. For non-fiction, discuss the major facts or ideas that the text contained.
- *Characterization:* Ask questions about the interest, motives, point of view, and feelings of real or fictional characters in the text.
- *Texts to Self:* Encourage students to make connections between the stories and themselves: their homes, neighborhoods, environment, families, feelings, and goals.

- *Self-questioning:* They can select three questions that they would like to answer about what they just read. They may want to select questions that can be answered in the story (literal questions) or go beyond the story (inferential questions). You'll be able to assess how well they are handling the text by the types of questions they are asking.

Another activity is to have them make a book commercial. As seen on countless television spots, they can make up a jingle, song, poem, slogan, or poster to advertise the book. They should give at least two reasons why people should read this book. They can also make a bookmark based on a scene from the story or a book jacket.

They can imagine interviewing a book character. For this exercise, have them choose an important character from the book and write sample interviewer's questions, "ask" the character questions about what happened in the story and write the character's answers. The student should answer the questions as he or she thinks the character would.

Additional activities connecting writing to literature or informational books are:

1. Write the events in the story on sentence strips and then sequence the events in a pocket chart or table.
2. Write a summary of the story highlights so others can see if they are interested in reading the book.
3. Try writing a short story based on the same genre as the book you just completed.
4. Turn a fable or fairy tale or other piece of science fiction around and write it as if it were true, for example, as you might read about it in your hometown daily newspaper.
5. Write an account of what you would have done if you were one of the main characters in the story instead of what the main character actually did.
6. Try writing a press release using the form found in the appendix.
7. Try writing a postcard to a friend describing the setting of the book and how you are visiting the place in the story for a vacation. Make sure you tell about the wonderful place you visited and what you saw and did. Write your short letter in the space given and on the other side, draw a picture of the setting (i.e., your vacation spot).

Another very helpful activity as an alternative to the ubiquitous book report is to have a child fill out a Mini–Book Report Form. The form is listed in Appendix A: It compresses the most important points on one or two pages and can be done in a relatively short time.

In order to strengthen their vocabulary, students can do these extra writing activities:

1. They can categorize words from their story by picking out twenty words and group them into four categories.
2. They can identify "feeling" words and categorize all words that show sorrow, anger, sadness, happiness, color, size, and so on. Or they can identify alternate words with the same meanings for common words such as "said" (e.g., exclaimed, replied), or alternate words that mean nice or good. They can develop their own word finders or specialized self-made dictionaries with theme words such as family words, sports words, food words, or unusual words; palindromes (words spelled the same forward and backward) such as mom; street words like avenue, boulevard, place, and cul-de-sac; or words that make a strong sound like *clap*, *bang*, or *crash*.
3. They can write about why the author selected a certain title for the book. They can write what they think the title of a particular book means before reading, and what they think about it after the reading is done. They can make up their own title if they think a different one would be better.
4. Students can find wonderful words that are unusual, weird sounding, confusing, or highly descriptive. They can use them in a sentence, tell why they picked them, and include the page number.

In addition to these activities, as students read a passage, you may stop them to record the main idea and map all facts they have learned up to the stopping point. This works well for children who have difficulty remembering an entire story or who tend to forget details. Use the T-Chart found in Appendix A to help students identify topic, main ideas, details, and sequence of events.

It is important to try to relate stories being read and discussed to students' own life experiences. Encourage students to make connections between the stories and themselves, their homes, neighborhoods, families, friends, pets, feelings, or life goals. Using story maps (see textbox 15.1) can also help a child gain greater understanding of text.

Make sure that students stop every so often and review the writing to see if they are indeed answering what must be answered. All too often a child finishes a piece of writing about baseball when indeed the task calls for an analysis of football. Children should review, revise, edit, and proofread if they have time during the test. Some tests give ample time for completing a planning page and response; this involves their ability to learn how to take notes (see chapter 11).

TEXTBOX 15.1 SAMPLE STORY MAP

Title: _____

Setting: _____

Characters: _____

Problem: _____

Event 1: _____

Event 2: _____

Event 3: _____

Event 4: _____

Event 5: _____

Solution: _____

Using poetry can also serve to excite and motivate children to read and write. It is often given on standardized reading tests for interpretation and analysis of figurative language. But poetry can fascinate and can touch children in deeper, more profound, and more meaningful ways. It can help them get in touch with their own images, feelings, and senses in their lives and the world around them. It can serve to promote greater writing capabilities because of this and enhance comprehension.

Have poetry books available and encourage students to select poems. They can read them, copy their favorite ones into a log, cut and paste poems from newspapers or magazines, or include their own poems in the log with accompanying sketches.

Tuck poems in your child's book bag to be read in school and at home. Have a 100-poem day when you celebrate the reading of the 100th poem. Poetry anthologies offer a wide variety of choices.

In addition to anthologies, you can choose to read poetry from this list of special poets:

- Langston Hughes
- Leland Jacobs
- Karla Kuskin
- Eve Merriam
- Lillian Moore
- Jack Prelutsky
- Shel Silverstein
- Charlotte Zolotow

Children can also listen to poems on tapes or make their own poetry tapes.

For yet another way to use poems, try the poetry activity shown in text-box 15.2. A student can write a poem by putting together the words from the chart in an interesting way.

TEXTBOX 15.2 WRITING A DESCRIPTIVE POEM

A descriptive poem uses details to paint pictures in a reader's mind. It tells how something looks, sounds, feels, smells, and tastes. Select a fragrant, unusual, or common food to discuss. Complete the poetry chart below:

Name of Food

Looks	*Sounds*	*Smells*	*Tastes*	*Feels*

An alternative is to try writing an "ABC poem." Have a child select a topic of interest, such as baseball. Use the order of the alphabet for arranging all the words in that poem. Use all of the letters. Pick one word for each letter. For instance, begin with the letter *a* and come up with a baseball word like *ace*, which means a fine player with great skills. When you come to *X* or *Z*, the student could form a word that contains the sound of the letter in it or create a nonsense word.

And certainly let's not forget the acrostic poem. Have the students use their names and write descriptive words about themselves. Thus, the boy's name Joe becomes

J—jovial O—outstanding B—exceptional

Another good activity involves the "Movie Review." Children frequently go to the movies so why not make good use of the experience by having them write movie critiques. They can first write a summary of what they saw and then write a critical analysis as movie reviewers do in newspapers. They can pretend they are movie critics working for their hometown newspaper and rate the movies they see on a 0–4 stars basis. Four stars, of course, being excellent.

Are zip lines the current fad? How about zip book bags. Teachers and parents can create book bags with accompanying suggestions on their use. Zip lock bags work very well. Parents can do the same on short or long car trips or especially if you are waiting on a long line at the bank, food-drive thru, or supermarket. Teachers and parents can keep track of these book bags by creating road map charts and by giving rewards as children reach a benchmark or milestone.

IDEA BANK

Have children write something relevant to themselves as well as in response to literature on a daily basis. The skill of writing can be equally as crucial as the skill of reading. In fact, it is more important.

Chapter Sixteen

Writing with the New Common Core Standards in Mind

There exists a paucity of good writing skills as demonstrated by our youth in schools, colleges, and in the workplace.

What sets good students apart from mediocre ones is not only their ability to read well, but to write competently. Teachers love students who can write well. They will get the better grades, because as far as college, high school, middle school, and elementary school is concerned, in addition to tests, students will be expected to do library or Internet research and write clear, concise, and competent follow-up essays and reports. Future employers love employees who can competently communicate in written discourse. They are the ones who will move ahead and get promoted.

The Common Core State Standards articulate the need for improved competency in writing across the board therefore it emphasizes various aspects of writing and the writing process itself. It is infinitely more important to master written discourse. This is what children need to do and that is to write clearly and capably involving their writing responses to literature, critical writing, drawing conclusions, writing summaries, writing arguments and persuasive essays, doing research, mastering the writing process approach, writing narratives and memoirs, and using technology to publish their writing. These are all common core goals. In addition, they need to refine their grammar, sentence structure, and spelling as well.

They will be called upon to demonstrate an opinion, judgment, and offer criticism. They will be asked to identify the topic and main idea, report on valid facts and pick out falsehoods, to determine fact from fiction, fact versus opinion, fantasy versus reality, and prove it by referring and quoting from the text. They will have to draw conclusions about information they collect.

Students must be able to speculate on future considerations of contemporary issues, reflect on them, and determine the outcomes, and how it affects society and individuals. They will be asked to extend their writing about a topic by doing further research using among other things the Internet. When writing narratives, they will be expected to fully describe their actions, behaviors, thoughts, and feelings.

When writing informational essays, they will be expected to use topic headers to help them organize the information. For example, topic headers about an essay on "Cats" can include:

- Why I Chose This Animal
- Cat Families
- Cat Colors and Markings
- Cat Breeds
- Cat Breeds I Prefer
- Cats From Around the World
- Cat Behavior
- Cat Movements
- Why Cats Make Good Pets
- Kitten Behaviors
- What Cats Eat and Drink
- Why Did the Egyptians Revere Cats?
- Cat Survival Outside the Home

Also, standards call for students to quote and use dialogue correctly and to state reasons in support of an issue. Furthermore, tests may call for students to write on a pre-selected topic or to have them write on some topic that they have knowledge about. Evaluators want to see how well your child uses transitional expression, such as however, nevertheless, moreover, etc. The test calls for using highly descriptive words and adjectives to convey and describe thoughts and ideas especially relating to characterization as well as avoiding trite words such as "good" or "bad."

In addition, what also may help to improve a student's writing is using the Internet in creating an on-line journal where an exchange of ideas and opinions, information, thoughts, or just plain gossip in the form of a web log or "blog" is attempted. The only pitfall to these digital quips is that they might be misused and lead to harsh criticism from other on-line students, bullying, sexual innuendo, threats, insults, and other anti-social activity. But a personal blog from student to student, when properly supervised can serve to create a valuable ongoing diary or commentary to communicate thoughts and feelings. Book reviews can be written, study aids and ideas discussed, journals, essays, poetry, etc., can be published.

A teacher and parent would have to take an enormous amount of time to monitor and control classroom, inter-classroom, and at home blogs, which might better be served by spending precious instructional time for conventional learning purposes. In my opinion, there are too many risks involved with creating personal blogs.

IDEA BANK

Writing is a key component toward developing literacy. It is a skill that must be reinforced at home as well as at school. Practice at locating and retrieving information in written text by teaching children how to use short quotes, long quotes, paraphrasing, and summarizing.

Chapter Seventeen

Keeping It Positive

Virtue is its own reward. Success is not about getting another video game, new bike, or money. Take a few minutes to think about how to handle praise, build self-respect, and boost morale. Every child needs to experience success and hear praise often. Consistent, well-placed, honest praise without qualification or equivocation is critical.

Praise encourages children to keep on trying to improve. It is equally important to tell children why you are praising them. Tell them exactly what they are doing that is positive. Be sure to reinforce and praise both successful and unsuccessful attempts when trying to figure out a word or an answer to a difficult question.

For instance, if a child repeats, stops, or returns to a word to try to fix it, then they should be praised for their attempts at self-correction. Enable them to experiment with this behavior. Self-corrections let you know that they are monitoring their own reading and that they notice when it does not sound right, look right, or make sense. Verbally praise them at every step:

- "Good job, you fixed your error all by yourself!"
- "I liked the way you read today, especially when I noticed you were really thinking about the story!"
- "You are definitely improving!"
- "Keep up the good work!"

Football players go crazy when they score a touchdown; they graphically and demonstratively portray their glee in many, sometimes unusual ways. But they do celebrate at every turn. Verbally praise every effort with a "Good Job!" Give stickers or points. Make up a certificate that children can display in their room. Chart their progress every day and display the chart as well. If a certain number of points is achieved, issue a certificate, buy them an ice cream cone or favorite candy, or have a pizza party.

Praise frequently and regularly. Smile. Children need a boost in ego to raise their levels of self-confidence, which is why some of our kids fall down and do not do well on standardized tests. Reading should be enjoyable. Sometimes a sincere expression of thanks like "Thank you for reading with me today," along with a hug or smile, goes a long way. Try praising them for being attentive, cooperative, reading with expression, or for just selecting an interesting story.

Planning for taking a standardized test is not unlike preparing for the big game. Coaches have playbooks, team executives are in the stands helping out, coaches wear headsets to communicate to their cohorts in the spy boxes, coaches have assistants to help them, and there are specialty teams and specialty trainers and physicians.

From the towel boy helping the players curtail their sweat and handing out drinks, everybody is doing their job. Players see videos of themselves, there are pregame and postgame meetings, and of course, there is practice, practice, and more practice. There is talk of team spirit, mixed with rugged individualism, but all for a common goal: to win.

If all the players come together—children, parents, teachers, school administrators, and school specialists—then success can and should be realized. Nothing less can be acceptable for our students.

IDEA BANK

Praise your child by giving oral praise and by rewarding via the use of progress charts, or rewarding good work with stickers, etc. Praise must be honest, well-meaning, and well-placed.

Chapter Eighteen

The Night Before

So what special thing should you do the night before a test? Nothing. That's what you do. Parents should do only normal everyday things around the house (if that's ever possible). They can cook a child's favorite meal and after that let the child finish homework, watch TV, or play video games. Children can also read for enjoyment.

They should go to bed early and in the morning, be sent off with a well-balanced nutritious breakfast, packing two #2 pencils in their book bag. No required reading, no preparation, no studying, no review. Parents should say as little as possible except for a few well-chosen words of encouragement. Everyone should really try to think of this day as just another school day.

If a child requires special testing conditions such as a school aide, a separate location, small group or individualized testing, or any other type of testing modification, make sure that that is in place prior to test day.

If a child becomes ill during the test, he or she should be removed from the test and retested another day. The same applies if a child should become upset for any reason. There are usually days set aside for makeups. If you find that a child freezes up during the administration of the test, ask for a makeup.

It is hoped that the testing conditions in the classroom are optimal, for example, sufficient lighting and a well-ventilated room. These variables can affect scores.

Children should know how to pace themselves and be aware of time. Tests are timed and the time limits should be told to the students as well as placed on the board for all to see, usually like this:

Table 18.1.

Name of Test	American Test of Reading Skills
Part I	Vocabulary
Test Begins	9:00 a.m.
Time of Test	20 minutes
Test Ends	9:20 a.m.

Children should wear a watch in case the school clock, usually in the front of the room, is not working or inaccurate. Sometimes the clocks in classrooms are either broken, too fast, or too slow.

Also, when a child selects a first answer, that answer should not be changed unless the child knows positively that an answer is in error. First instincts are important. Children should stick to their first original choice. They should try to complete the entire test, answering every question. If they are running out of time, they should guess, and if they are almost out of time, they should just fill in one blank circle for each question left on their answer grids.

Remind children to be careful when reading the directions. They can ask for clarification and a rereading if they do not understand any direction. If a child gets stuck on a question, suggest that he or she move on to the next one. The child can return to that question after answering everything else.

Parents should receive an objective report of their child's test results in a few months.

IDEA BANK

Just be the model of what calm and reassuring is. Your child needs this and needs your full support at this critical time.

Chapter Nineteen

Getting the Results

Within a few months, the school or school district, via mail, will send a report of the child's results. It may be attached to the report card. The notification should explain how a student performed and may contain other evaluative information. Results can be expressed in many different ways according to the test parameters, district formulas, state guidelines, and test manufacturers' specifications.

Results of standardized tests should be used as points for analysis in the improvement of a child's instruction and not only for promotional considerations and class placement. Educators should have a thorough understanding of the nature of the test, its uses, its limitations, and how they can best interpret test results and explain them to parents. Tests are merely a work sample of a child's learnings.

A reading achievement test may measure the ability to understand words in context, the ability to identify the main thought in a passage, and the ability to comprehend inferentially and literally. But it cannot measure everything a child has learned; therefore, a complete picture of what was actually learned is not readily obtained.

Keep in mind that these tests do not measure intellect. They measure whatever has developed in a child's school learning ability. They measure mastered skills in an effort to better understand a child's instructional needs.

Other information about a child should always be used in addition to test results in order to make reasonably informed, rational, and sound educational decisions. The school should assess a child's progress and achievement using teacher-made tests, student-made tests, portfolio assessment, projects, attendance, class participation, cooperative learning and group projects, teacher observation, and conferencing.

Checklists and monitoring logs can also fill in the picture of a child's overall achievement. These assessments are ongoing and are done daily, weekly, and monthly throughout the school year.

A test score shows how well a child performed, but it cannot reveal why. Tests reflect prior learning experiences, cumulative knowledge, memory, awareness of test orientation, preparation, structure, and inherited traits at the time of testing. We know that some children are good test takers; others are not.

Every test score is an approximation, not an exact score of a child's capabilities. A child's actual score may fall into (or be reported as falling between) a range of scores. The scores should not be perceived as good or bad. But you know they usually are. The score is an indication of a level of performance in relation to a general test population such as a national sample group.

It is a measurement based on what others have done across the country in that same grade and age level. It would not be fair to take one set of test results on one given day and use it to label a child as an underachiever.

A competent teacher will take the results and use them in a positive way for the planning and improvement of future instruction. Parents must try to make sure that this is being done, otherwise, test results are a waste of time. A low score, should a child receive one, should be interpreted very carefully. A low score indicates that a child scored below an average range at a particular point in time. It does not mean that with proper help, he or she cannot score in that range or even higher.

The effectiveness of any educational program should not be measured solely on standardized test results. School performance, as well as a child's individual performance, is affected by the cumulative effect of instruction as well as many extraneous factors such as pupil attendance, mobility, motivation for learning, family socioeconomic background, parental interest in academic achievement, peer pressures and influences, family lifestyle, and the level of verbal communication in the home.

Yet, obviously some children have an innate ability to do well on tests with little studying, no parental influence, and little teacher impact.

A score report should state a child's name, class, school, date of test, teacher's name, and other basic data. Be prepared to see many different types of scores on the score report. Results are first reported as a *raw score*. The raw score is the exact number of question items answered correctly on a given test or subtest. This score will be converted to a developmental score for analysis and interpretation. The *percent correct score* is the number of correct responses divided by the number of questions in a given test or subtest.

Another figure you will see is the *percentile rank*. This is used to report a child's standing in comparison to all other students who were tested in the national sample. The scale ranges from 1–99 and shows the percentage of students who earned higher or lower test scores.

For instance, if a child earned a percentile rank of 60 on a particular test, it means that he or she scored better than 60 percent of all of the students in the norm group. Conversely, it means that 40 percent of those pupils scored as well or better than that child. These scores are fluid and differ from group to group and at various times of the year. A child can be in more than one group and achieve a different percentile rank score in each group.

Norms can be derived from a number of reference groups, which might include large metropolitan city schools, private schools, or particular socioeconomic districts. Local norms are a percentile rank derived from your child's local district population rather than from a national sample. This may be helpful in analyzing and interpreting a child's test performance when a school district's population varies greatly from the national sample.

The only scores that are really looked at by teachers are the developmental or growth scores, called the *grade equivalent*. The grade equivalent is based on the reported raw score; it indicates the grade level at which a typical student makes this raw score. A score of 2.1 is interpreted as the first digit (2) being the grade (second grade) and the second digit (1) being the month within the grade.

For example, if a student gets a grade equivalent of 4.7, this means that the raw score on the test is the same as that made by the typical or average student in the fourth grade at the end of seven months. If a student makes a grade equivalent of 6.0, this means that the test performance equals that of a typical student just beginning sixth grade.

It is important to note that grade equivalent scores are not directly related to a specific school district curriculum. This score is merely an estimate of where a child is along a developmental path. Grade-equivalent scores are helpful only when used and interpreted correctly. They can serve to indicate the developmental level of a child's performance. They can be averaged for purposes of making group comparisons. They are suitable for measuring individual growth.

Once again, test scores should never be interpreted in isolation, but in conjunction with other forms of alternative assessment and conventional tests. A standardized test can only measure a sample of the curriculum. Test results show the level of achievement but cannot explain why a child performed this way. Low scores should always be analyzed with extreme care. If a parent needs an explanation of a child's test results, then they should make an appointment with the teacher or principal and have them explain it.

It is not a good idea to compare one child with another. Growth, achievement, and developmental patterns are different for every child. You must not expect a slower student to grow as rapidly as a student who is a high achiever. Every child is unique. Let the statistics speak for themselves. The big job lies ahead.

Teachers and parents must work closely to plan the next steps, selecting an appropriate enrichment, remedial, corrective, supplementary, or compensatory program. The test should help the teacher pinpoint and isolate any trouble spots.

Tests also have what they call *standard deviation*, which means that there is a variance or spread of scores within a particular group. A related statistic, *standard error*, measures how reliable the test is. If standardized tests were to be repeatedly given, a student's score would not be exactly the same every time, but it would fall into a general range. So, like other tests and assessments, these tests are not totally accurate.

We can never get away from standardized tests. They will always be with us. Try to encourage and praise a child's efforts no matter what the scores reveal. It is important that teachers and parents stay positive and conscientious and plan for a better educational future for a child. Do not let the child know that you are disappointed. This can only lead to a child's diminution of his image as a person as well as his confidence.

In the end, it is important to remember that the Pinpoint Reading program should continue no matter what the scores reveal. Literacy is a lifelong skill, and for some, it is a struggle to obtain. A child is a lifelong learner and needs support. So whatever time you decide to spend on helping your child read and write better, double it, no, triple it.

IDEA BANK

If you are not sure about how to interpret results, see your child's teacher or principal for insight and a full explanation.

Chapter Twenty

A Pinpoint Reading Bibliography

CLASSICS

Aesop	Aesop's Fables (many versions)
Andersen, Hans Christian	Andersen's fairy tales (many versions)
Barrie, J. M.	*Peter Pan*
Carroll, Lewis	*Alice's Adventures in Wonderland*
	Through the Looking Glass
DeFoe, Daniel	*Robinson Crusoe*
Doyle, Sir Arthur Conan	Sherlock Holmes mysteries
Irving, Washington	*Rip Van Winkle*
Pyle, Howard	*The Merry Adventures of Robin Hood*
Sewell, Anna	*Black Beauty*
Stevenson, Robert Lewis	*Treasure Island*
Swift, Jonathan	*Guilliver's Travels*
Travers, P. L.	*Mary Poppins*
Twain, Mark	*The Adventures of Tom Sawyer*
White, E. B.	*Charlotte's Web*
Wilder, Laura Ingalls	*Little House on the Prairie*
Wyss, Johann David	*The Swiss Family Robinson*

PRIMARY

Grades 2 and 3

Adler, David A.	Cam Jansen mysteries
Blume, Judy	*Freckle Juice*
Byars, Betsy Cromer	*The Joy Boys*
Christopher, Matt	*The Dog That Called the Pitch*
Cowley, Joy	*Agapanthus Hum and the Eyeglasses*
Giff, Patricia Reilly	*Watch Out, Ronald Morgan!*
Hurwitz, Johanna	*Ever-Clever Elisa*
Rylant, Cynthia	*In Aunt Lucy's Kitchen*
Sachar, Louis	Marvin Redpost books
Spinelli, Jerry	*Blue Ribbon Blues*

Grades 3 and 4

Auch, Mary Jane	*I Was a Third Grade Science Project*
Blume, Judy	*Tales of a Fourth Grade Nothing*
Cameron, Ann	*The Stories Julian Tells*
Cleary, Beverly	*Ramona's World*
Dahl, Roald	*James and the Giant Peach*
Hurwitz, Johanna	*Class Clown*
Le Guin, Ursula K.	*Catwings*
MacLachlan, Patricia	*Sarah, Plain and Tall*
Osborne, Mary Pope	*Standing in the Light*
Scieszka, Jon	*Your Mother Was a Neanderthal*
Smith, Robert Kimmel	*Chocolate Fever*

Grades 5 and 6

Avi	*The Barn*
Blume, Judy	*Here's to You, Rachel Robinson*
Bunting, Eve	*Spying on Miss Muller*
Byars, Betsy	*The Summer of the Swans*
Cleary, Beverly	*Dear Mr. Henshaw*
Conrad, Pam	*Stonewords: A Ghost Story*
Fox, Paula	*Monkey Island*
Henkes, Kevin	*Words of Stone*
Lowry, Lois	*Number the Stars*
Paterson, Katherine	*Bridge to Terabithia*
Speare, Elizabeth George	*The Sign of the Beaver*

Grades 7 and 8

Almond, David	*Kit's Wilderness*
Anderson, Laurie Halse	*Speak*
Avi	*The Good Dog*
Brashares, Ann	*The Sisterhood of the Traveling Pants*
Cooper, Susan	*King of Shadows*
Klass, David	*California Blue*
Konigsburg, E. L.	*Silent to the Bone*
Lowry, Lois	*Gathering Blue*
Sones, Sonya	*What My Mother Doesn't Know*
Taylor, Mildred D.	*Roll of Thunder, Hear My Cry*

These lists are short; you can obtain more extensive ones at your local library, school library, or through the Internet. Do not forget the summer months when children are out of school. Continue the program and enroll them in one of many summer reading programs sponsored by your local community public library or your child's school.

Some educators think that if children do not read during the summer months they lose ground. Research has shown this to be true, so reading all year round is a good rule and routine to follow. Pinpoint Reading does not take a vacation.

IDEA BANK

The best book is not on any list. It is the book your child is interested in and wants to read.

Chapter Twenty-One

Using EBooks

Cuddling up with a book, whether it be soft cover or hard is a wonderfully tactile experience. The proliferation of eBooks which can be obtained from online libraries and online sellers of electronic books and readers is something that can be extremely beneficial to your child in and out of school. EBooks can be purchased and quickly downloaded to your child's eBook reading device in a fast and extremely convenient way. A flip of one's finger can take you to new and exciting reading adventures. Certainly, in today's electronic milieu, eBooks and readers have become very user friendly.

The reason for this is simple. Children are able to choose titles within seconds. They can adjust the size of the page, they can automatically return a child to a page that they missed or had just stopped on, and they can allow children to take notes as they read as well as emphasize text by highlighting certain portions of the story. EReaders can allow children to add drawings, assist in text read alouds, and they come with built-in dictionaries. Transportability is a key issue and kids can take them anywhere. An eReader can enable a child to carry many stories in one machine and is only limited to the amount of memory it has capability of.

Also, many eReaders can now be used to connect to the Internet and can accept other applications as needed and warranted.

While you are busy cooking dinner or while a teacher is working with one small focus group, eBooks serve to allow for individualized instruction in reading and can help to reinforce critical reading skills involving comprehension and word analysis.

The electronic age has arrived and is here to stay and further refinements to the already existing fleet of eBooks and ePads are already being developed with even greater capabilities.

IDEA BANK

The use of eBooks is an important variation to reading that your child should be exposed to especially on those short or long car trips or vacations at the seashore.

Chapter Twenty-Two

Making Literature Come Alive

Sometimes art can facilitate learning and understanding of textual material. It can facilitate in the active construction or reconstruction of meaning, organization of knowledge, and retrieval and storage of information. Pictures, sketches, illustrations, drawings, even doodling provide an opportunity to interact with the content to gain an in-depth understanding of the material being read.

Try using various media such as poster paint, watercolors, chalk, colored pencils, markers, pastels, charcoal, pencils, crayons, or even finger paints. Encourage your students to create pictures that represent their understanding and interpretation of the key concepts, ideas, or facts. They can discuss through their pictures what the story was about. They can write a brief summary of the material after they have completed their art projects. Display their completed projects in their rooms.

ACTIVITY 1

Purpose: To analyze the content of a story based on a personal response to literature by engaging in the personal construction of meaning.

Product: Sketches of the part a student liked best, such as the most exciting or funniest part, a beginning or concluding scene, a surprise ending, an unusual object, or a fascinating character.

Process: Students sketch a picture that represents their understanding of the key concepts, ideas, or facts from a book, and then explain the material sketched.

ACTIVITY 2

Purpose: To use knowledge of the structure of a story to reconstruct the order of critical events.

Product: A filmstrip showing the major sequence of events from a story.

Process: Students draw a series of filmstrips showing the sequence of significant events from a story. On the bottom of each frame of the filmstrip, students write a caption that describes the scene. They then read and discuss the filmstrips.

ACTIVITY 3

Purpose: To interpret the details and actions depicted in a cartoon strip and reconstruct the plot by creating new dialogue in coordination with the existing art.

Product: A new story line and a recreated cartoon.

Process: Students cut out the conversation balloons of their favorite cartoon from the Sunday comic section of the newspaper and place the cartoon onto white construction paper. They fill the empty balloons with new dialogue based on their ideas for an original cartoon story. They can first practice writing dialogue to determine whether it makes sense throughout the comic strip and creates a clear, coherent story.

ACTIVITY 4

Purpose: To identify the setting or multiple settings in a story using a student's knowledge of the story elements.

Product: An illustrated map depicting the location(s) where the story took place.

Process: Students draw an illustrated map of the setting of the story depicting the main locations of towns, buildings, shops, homes of main characters, spots where action took place, main roads, and geographical features relevant to the plot of the story. Students then write a detailed explanation of the setting based on their map, how the setting was instrumental to the plot, and why the author chose that particular place.

ACTIVITY 5

Purpose: To synthesize information, facts, and details about the story by designing an advertisement.

Product: A poster and marketing strategy to "sell" the book to other classmates.

Process: On poster board, students illustrate an attention-grabbing scene from the story they just read and write an inviting caption that will entice people to buy the book. In addition, they should develop, in writing, a market strategy for the book they are trying to sell.

ACTIVITY 6

Purpose: To demonstrate understanding of the story by writing a short summary of the pertinent main ideas and supporting details and by researching the author's life.

Product: A colorful and informative book jacket.

Process: Using construction paper, students design a front cover for the book that is inviting and captures the imagination of the reader. On the inside left-hand flap that is folded to about three inches, the students write a brief summary of the book without divulging too many relevant details that will give the plot away. The students should read some sample flaps as models for writing. On the right-hand flap, the students write a short biography of the author's life and include other books that the author has written. To ham it up and legitimize the cover, have the students add contrived recommendation blurbs from fictitious reviewers or organizations.

ACTIVITY 7

Purpose: To interpret and apply an author's use of figurative language as students use similes, metaphors, or idiomatic expressions to develop poetry based upon their reading of tall tales, poetry, fables, and so on.

Product: A decorative T-shirt with a poem, slogan, phrase, or thematic statement that contains some type of figurative language.

Process: Using a white T-shirt and a permanent set of color markers, students create poetry and illustrations to decorate their T-shirt.

ACTIVITY 8

Purpose: To apply knowledge of the structure of a story to construct a series of illustrations.

Product: A mini-mural that depicts the events that occurred at the beginning, middle, and end of a story.

Process: On a large sheet of construction paper folded into three parts, students paint a mini-mural using crayons, markers, colored pencils, or paint showing the important events in the story in sequential order. On the bottom of each frame, students write a description of what each scene represents.

ACTIVITY 9

Purpose: To define the main idea or theme of a book by applying their knowledge in creating an illustration.

Product: An oversized commemorative postage stamp reflecting the main idea, main event, or other chosen aspect of the story.

Process: Using a large piece of construction paper with precut serrated edges resembling those of a postage stamp, students illustrate a scene from the story that portrays the main theme of the book or some relevant aspect of a character's life. The students should see what actual commemorative postage stamps look like to get some idea of how to design the project.

ACTIVITY 10

Purpose: To create and affirm the importance and enjoyment of reading.

Product: A bookmark that serves as an incentive and affirmation for reading.

Process: Students create a Pinpoint Reading bookmark using a slogan that serves as an incentive to read. For instance, they can create a slogan or expression such as "Be A Busy Bee—Read!" with an accompanying artistic rendering.

ACTIVITY 11

Purpose: To use specific evidence from the story read to describe main characters.

Product: A calendar representing a book completed for that month.

Process: Have students decorate a calendar for each month showing the dates with the appropriate holidays and special occasions.

Leave enough blank space on top and split the space in two equal parts. On one side, draw a picture of the main character, and on the adjacent side, write a descriptive paragraph about the behavioral traits and attributes the character typifies.

ACTIVITY 12

Purpose: To identify the main idea and supporting details in a story.

Product: A main-idea mobile.

Process: Students make a mobile by drawing pictures illustrating the main idea and the important supporting details. First, have them draw pictures on poster board and cut them out. (They can draw on both sides.) Then have them make a sign that tells the name of the book, the author's name, and the main idea with an accompanying picture. Next, have them attach a piece of string to each drawing showing an important detail. Finally, have them tie each string to a clothes hanger and attach it to the ceiling.

ACTIVITY 13

Purpose: To understand the events in a story and place them in a logical sequential order to develop a simple retelling/summary.

Product: A flipbook showing the sequence of major events in a story.

Process: Have students fold a large piece of paper lengthwise in half and cut three slits of equal length from the top piece. Your child can draw on each flap what happened in the beginning, middle, and end of the story. As they flip up each flap, they write underneath what actually happened in their own words.

ACTIVITY 14

Purpose: To apply knowledge gained from reading a story to identify important details.

Product: A "triarama" illustrating an important event from the story.

Process: Another interesting art project is creating an alternative to the shoebox diorama, called the "triarama." After cutting and gluing the triarama, children decorate the inside with cutouts and crayon sketches that depict a critical scene from a book. They then attach a 3 × 5 index card to the bottom lip of the triarama that describes the scene above it.

ACTIVITY 15

Purpose: To use evidence from the story to describe characters, their motivation, and their positive and negative traits.

Product: Coffee can art.

Process: Decorate a coffee can with the face and type of clothing worn by the main character. Inside the can, place important details of the character's life on 3 × 5 index cards (one fact per card), such as where she was born, the foods she ate, or her accomplishments.

ACTIVITY 16

Purpose: To critically analyze, synthesize, and evaluate the information obtained within a story to create a cogent written response.

Product: A newsletter.

Process: After reading a story, produce a newsletter with the following features:

1. News features about events that happened in the story
2. Interviews with major characters, the author, illustrator, and so on
3. Weather reports for the setting of the stories
4. A TV guide listing fictitious programs about the story (e.g., a miniseries)
5. Letters to the editor from key characters
6. Ads for a movie based on the book
7. A song or poem inspired from the movie
8. Crossword puzzles made from key vocabulary words collected from the story

ACTIVITY 17

Purpose: To use the knowledge of story structure and events to write an extended response.
Product: A sequel.
Process: Children might like to plan a sequel to a story they have read. Have them plan how long after the original story the sequel takes place and identify the main plot and events. Have them write an outline first, stating the setting, characters, and plot.

ACTIVITY 18

Purpose: To draw conclusions and inferences about characters and use evidence to describe characters.
Product: A story map.
Process: Have students map a journey taken by a character in a story. Write a map with pictures, roads, and places visited with a map key to show the journey pathways and other special roads. Follow up with a discussion, which would include the following questions:

- What was the purpose of the character's journey?
- Was there a search for something special?

- What was the character like at the start of his journey?
- How did the character's attitude or feelings change by the end of the trip?
- What special events took place along the way that were significant to the characters?
- Did the main characters ever reach their destinations?
- Are they still trying to find how to get there?
- Were there any possible roadblocks in the way of living their lives?

ACTIVITY 19—READING RECIPES

In this fun extracurricular activity, children will be given the opportunity to read and interpret recipes that they will actually cook with their parents or teachers.

Before Cooking:

1. Tell your child that they will bake cookies and that they will read the recipe first.
2. Go over the details of what a recipe contains.
3. Have your child read aloud the different sections of the recipe.
4. Ask your child to determine the different parts of the recipe and how they should prepare for baking.
5. Go over the specific recipe and by drawing attention to the original, compare and contrast the original one with the revised recipe that is included.
6. Review procedures again, preparing the necessary measuring spoons, bowls, stirring spoons, etc.

During Cooking:

The child will call out and measure and then set aside all ingredients as called for in the recipe.

Erica's Chocolate Chip Cookies

Original Recipe:

2 cups flour
1 teaspoon baking soda
1 teaspoon salt
1 cup butter
1 cup sugar
1 cup brown sugar
2 eggs
12 ounces semi-sweet chocolate chips
1 teaspoon vanilla extract

Revised Recipe:

2 cups flour
1 teaspoon baking soda
½ teaspoon salt
½ cup margarine
⅔ cup sugar
2 eggs
6 ounces semi-sweet chocolate chips
1 teaspoon vanilla extract
½ cup raisins

Vocabulary:

Semi-sweet: discuss what "semi" means and make a list of other "semi" words
Extract—how else is this word used.
Raisins—talk about how raisins are grown and made.
Vanilla—How is it made and used?
Chocolate—Where do we get this from? Talk about the countries that grow the bean.

Procedures:

1. Preheat oven to 375 degrees F.
2. In a small bowl, combine flour, baking soda, and salt; set aside.
3. In a large bowl, combine butter, sugar, brown sugar, and vanilla extract; beat until creamy with a wooden spoon.
4. Beat in eggs.
5. Gradually add flour mixture.
6. Stir in chocolate chips.
7. Drop the cookie dough by teaspoon onto an ungreased cookie sheet.
8. Bake for 9 to 11 minutes. How can you tell if they are done?

After Cooking:

1. Write in a "Chef's Journal" how the cookie looks, tastes, feels, smells, etc. Describe the color, shape, size, softness, texture, etc.
2. Describe in your journal how hard or easy it was, any problems encountered, and how they were solved. What would you add to the recipe to make it taste different or change the shape, etc?
3. Children can begin to save their favorite recipes in a cookbook whether they have actually cooked them or have a desire to in the future.

IDEA BANK

Do not forget to try other recipes that your child might like, especially the ones cooked around holiday time. Also trips to museums and art galleries can further enhance a child's creative spirit. If children are not inclined to favor art, then using cutouts, collages, and stick-figure drawings can suffice. Here, the process of reading and creating is as important as the final product itself.

Chapter Twenty-Three

A Troubleshooting Guide

Reading is the process of constructing meaning from written texts. It is a very complex skill that involves the coordination of a number of specific behaviors that must fall into place for reading to become efficient. A child's language is a composite of three systems: semantics, which is reading for meaning; syntax, which is understanding the effect that grammar and sentence structure have on our ability to understand print; and *graphophonics*, which involves the letter/sound correspondence (phonics) that is the basis for decoding words.

Learning to read involves an admixture and coordination of these three cueing systems. Since reading is a complex process and can be taught in many different ways, there is no one process that works best. Children use cues and strategies to help them unlock the concepts of print and the meaning of text.

The first system, meaning or semantics, is based on a child's prior knowledge and sense of a story. Meaning cues also come from the text and pictures in the story. As children read, they should ask themselves: Does it make sense? For example, if a sentence in a story says, "The cat was little and cute," and a child reads it as, "The cat was little and cut," but then changes "cut" to "cute," a child has used meaning to self-correct because what the child first read did not make sense.

Another system involves the use of sentence structure and grammar (syntax) that is based on a child's understanding of grammar patterns, language structure, and the English language. Structural cues can also come from a child's own natural language. A student should think as they read: Does it sound right? For example, a sentence might read "This is my kitten," but a child reads it as "This is my kangaroo." In order to correct this miscue or mistake, a child must learn to focus on a visual strategy to figure out the word. Certainly the word *kangaroo* fits grammatically, but it does not sound right.

The last system, graphophonics, uses visual or graphic cues based on a child's knowledge of letter-sound relationships and print. Visual cues also come from a child's knowledge of letters and words. For example, your child might read a sentence by saying, "John lives in a horse," when the sentence really says, "John lives in a house." A proficient reader would then ask: Does it look right to me? Sometimes children just look at the first sound, avoiding the rest of the word and ignoring the meaning altogether.

Children must independently use all three systems within the reading process and develop a variety of strategies if they are to become successful readers. These systems cannot and should not be taught in isolation. Learning to read requires cooperation, intensive phonics knowledge, sharing interaction, experiences, and a strong collaborative effort between the parent, teacher, and child.

Placing the importance on reading for meaning or comprehension is paramount to understanding the printed word. In addition, reading for appreciation and enjoyment will eventually lead to the development of competent readers and writers.

Learning to read and write involves purposeful, relevant, well-planned, and appropriately-leveled activities that are closely related to the needs of the student. Reading education should involve experiences that are cross-curricular and interdisciplinary as well as thematic and all-encompassing, enabling the child to experience other curriculum areas such as social studies, history, science, math, and so on.

Reading skills can be taught systematically where needed and warranted, but can also be taught as the need arises in direct relationship with the literature being used. Although state standards cannot possibly cover every possible behavior to be learned, relevant applicable standards must be addressed and reflected in every well-planned unit or lesson activity.

Reading, writing, and language arts are interrelated skills and should be taught in a unified interdisciplinary approach. Having immediate access to high-quality literature promotes success in reading and sustaining children in becoming lifelong learners of literature. Above all else, fostering love and appreciation of reading and literature is crucial.

You might ask yourself, What does a competent, skilled reader do while reading a book? How do they act? What does it look like? First, skilled readers are self-monitoring their reading as they go through the text to determine when they are or are not processing the material. They stop and question what they do not understand.

Competent readers will usually recall what they already know about the topic before, during, and after they have read. As they read, their knowledge base expands. Competent readers also know how to skim, scan, summarize, and extricate information from the reading material not only for test taking, but also to do research or just for their own pleasure or need to know. They learn how to assimilate, synthesize, summarize, and evaluate the material.

As they read, they question. They ponder what the author had in mind when writing a story and the message behind it. They also know how to draw inferences and conclusions and make predictions as they actively interpret reading material.

Good readers constantly upgrade their understanding and reassess what they have read. Readers who share an image of what they have read show greater understanding, which leads to enjoyment and appreciation of reading.

Proficient readers learn to correct mistakes. They use their skills to reread, retell, and rediscover what they are reading about. But it is all for the purpose of reading and understanding the printed word. Equally critical is the need to develop greater fluency in reading because if fluency is smooth and flawless, children's ability to read for meaning is enhanced.

Sometimes these behaviors do not take place or fit together to form a flow of understanding and learning. Some pieces of the reading puzzle need to be reworked and retrofitted when problems arise. This guide involves the self-correction of general word attack, word identification problems, and comprehension issues that you can identify, address, and remediate on the spot.

Here are some quick and easy tips for fixing reading problems:

Tracking

Children who have trouble with tracking are unable to follow the printed word in a given sentence. They lose their place and skip over words and whole sentences.

Do this: Show the child how to finger-track from word to word and from sentence to sentence. The child can use a ruler, but avoid the plastic see-through ones as they can cause confusion. Another method is to use an index card, which is placed below the line of print being read. Continue until you are able to observe a gain in skill and confidence. Then remove the devices and see what happens. If there is a return of the problem, re-introduce the above measures.

Fluency

A student struggling with fluency reads very slowly, laboriously, and word by word. He or she extensively pauses between words, leaving a gap and not allowing words to flow smoothly and continuously. Words do not flow as they would as if you were talking to someone. The student may also lack confidence, or the reading material may be too difficult.

Do this: Model how good reading should sound with pauses and into-nation. Be expressive and enunciate every word. Try repeated readings of the same sentence until the child is familiar with how whole sentences should be read. You model, then the child reads. Or read aloud together, taking turns reading the sentence until mastery is attained ("mastery" is usually defined as three trials with no mistakes).

You can also use somewhat easier material until fluency increases. Model what good reading and fluency sounds like using inflections and expressive speech. Start the child out by giving them easier books to read and do repeated readings with him or her. Graduate to more difficult, chal-lenging material. Have the child focus on the whole sentence by blocking out the rest of the passage with an index card or ruler.

Another approach is to have the child write his or her own story or dictate a story to you as you write it down. Being familiar with one's own language via story dictation can improve fluency. Dictated stories are individualized and personalized, developed with children on a one-to-one basis.

You can prompt a child who has difficulty in dictating a story by asking, "What happened next?" "Can you tell me more?" or "How do you feel about it?" Then read the dictated story back to the child, twice-modeling fluency. The child reads and then rereads the story several times. Children can select several words that gave them trouble during the dictation and use flash cards as an aid in pronunciation. Flash cards are made on 3 × 5 index cards. Follow this procedure:

Flash the words for a few seconds.
If a child gets the word correct, place it in a "correct word" pile.
If a child gets a word wrong, help the child pronounce it, then put it back
   in the deck for quick review.
Any incorrect word must be given three trials or flashes.
Try to achieve three consecutive positive responses (indicating mastery)
   in order for the word to be placed in the "correct word" pile.

Another way to improve fluency is to play the game known as Concentration:

Turn over the flash cards.
Ask the child to guess which card contains a particular word.
Turn the card over to reveal the word.
If it is correct, leave the word showing; if not, turn the card back over.
Continue the game until all words are recognized.

You can also use a cassette tape with reading material. Play only one passage at a time, maybe just a sentence. Then increase to two sentences, and then to a full paragraph. Yet another approach is to do repeated listening using the following method:

Have the child listen to one sentence.
Rewind and listen again.
The child then repeats the sentence from memory, or the child speaks
   along as he or she listens to the tape without the book.
The child then listens to the sentence while reading it in the text.
Repeat the previous step.
The child then reads the sentence alone, without the tape.
Repeat if necessary.
Go on to another sentence and repeat the process.

Here are a few more suggestions for helping a child improve fluency:

Echo read: You say it, and then the child says it.
Choral read: Read the piece aloud together. But do not allow finger-tracking as it can slow the pace down.

Sometimes, using short poetry selections can help promote fluency with repeated readings.

Run-On Reading

"Run-on reading" is when a child reads too fast and fails to stop for punctuation, ignoring periods and commas.

Do this: Model passages with commas and periods. Review what periods and commas do. Tell your child that a period acts like a stop sign for the driver. A comma is like a yield sign, indicating that you have to slow down a bit but not stop completely. Try breaking down a sentence and read its phrases. Use different colors for each phrase.

Mispronunciations

When a child continually pronounces words incorrectly, you should consider that the reason may be poor phonics knowledge, or the child is not using the tools he or she has learned to decode words. However, it is also wise to make sure the child's sight and hearing are adequate.

If you suspect a physical problem, a doctor's examination should be done to rule out an auditory or visual problem that might be responsible for the reading difficulty. Sometimes children read too fast and do not pay adequate attention. Carelessness and speed often lead to mispronunciation.

Do this: In order to help children improve their word attack skills, you may decide to buy some commercially-prepared phonics games purchased at toy stores, educator supply stores, or on-line dealers. You can also find these games at regular bookstores.

Here are some other ideas:

Make lists of certain letter combinations that have the same sounds such as *at*.

Make a list of troublesome prefixes and suffixes, such as *re-* or *-ful*, and review them on flash cards.

Make a word box filled with index cards of those hard-to-pronounce words found in their daily reading.

Have them ladder words like *at—bat—bats—batting—batted—batter—battery*, and so on.

Another idea is to substitute a different letter to add to a word that they have trouble with. For example, if a child is having trouble with the word *bent*, have the child make a list with similar sounding words such as *sent*, *rent*, and *went*. Do the same thing with a word like *smart*. Then give the child a number of words ending in *-art* like *chart*, *cart*, and so on.

Model how to sound out words. Ask a child to think about a mispronounced word by stopping right then and there and asking, "Does that make sense?" Repeat the incorrect sound and say, "You said this but what should it really sound like?" or "Try to say it again."

Sometimes covering the difficult word and have students guess it, or framing the word to have their eyes focus more directly on it can be beneficial. Also, cover up parts of the word and help them say it, then reveal more parts as you go along.

Skipping Over Words

When students omit certain words or even whole phrases or sentences, they are not being as careful as they should. Sometimes it just might be caused by poor reading habits. However, it could also be caused by inadequate word attack skills.

Do this: Call attention to the problem immediately when it occurs. Use a ruler to track each line. If an omission is found, have the child repeat the line three times. Discontinue use of ruler if the problem subsides. If tracking continues to be a problem, have the child temporarily use a finger to track while reading.

Repeats Words Frequently

If a child constantly rereads the same word or phrase, he or she may be exhibiting poor word recognition skills or it may be caused by developing a bad habit over the years without corrective measures.

Do this: Tell the child about the repeated word. Chorally read (i.e., read aloud together) the sentence first. Then have the child reread it alone. If necessary, have the child pace him- or herself, using a finger on a temporary basis, until the problem clears up. You can also provide easier reading material in which the words present no problem. Break the habit.

Insertions

"Insertions" means that a child adds words that are not present within the sentence. Sometimes this occurs due to plain carelessness, anxiety to read better, or an attempt to read more quickly. Sometimes it is a bad habit to add words that may or may not interfere with comprehension.

Do this: Point out each unwanted addition in the sentence. If it does not really interfere with comprehension, just point it out and say, "Are you sure it says that?" Then reread. Chorally read the sentence together, then let them reread it again by themselves.

Substitutions

Some children substitute one word for another when reading. Usually due to carelessness, children may read one word and substitute another of similar meaning. Also, substitutions which are not contextually correct are usually caused by word recognition difficulties.

Do this: Reread and point out mistakes immediately.

Basic Sight Words Not Known

A child might be unable to read some of what are known as "sight words," words that are commonly used and known in most reading material. These words appear frequently enough that it is essential that a child recognize them instantly without having to resort to using phonics. If they cannot recognize these words, their fluency suffers.

Do this: Keep a basic sight-word box filled with index cards. Write the unknown word on one side, and write a sentence using that word on the other side. Sound the word out first, when possible, because some words are so irregular that they do not sound as they are spelled. But then, after that first reading, it should no longer be sounded out. Flash words every day until mastered. You can also develop sentences with the key word removed, then have the child fill in the blanks with the appropriate basic sight word.

You can play the *WORDO* game (see chapter 8), a bingo-like game in which you call out the word and your child attempts to correctly identify the word on a card of basic sight words they have trouble identifying. Play several games, switching cards frequently.

Guesses at Words

A child might guess at unfamiliar words instead of correctly identifying them. This may be due to poor word attack skills, phonics knowledge, or inability to take a word apart. The child also may not be able to use contextual clues as he or she reads.

Do this: Stop and talk about the word that was guessed at. Help the child analyze the word by sounding it out together. This will get the child into the habit of analyzing mistakes. Help the child to sound out the first sound, second, third, and so on. Then give them help in putting those sounds together. Ask, "Does this word make sense?" Ask them to reread the sentence which contained the guessed at word for accuracy and fluency.

Weak Structural Analysis Skills

Structural analysis skill refers to a child's ability to decode or analyze a word through the study of roots, prefixes, suffixes, word beginnings, endings, word families, plurals, possessives, compound words, syllable separation and identification, and identification of "chunks" in words. A child may be able to unlock the pronunciation of a word through phonics, but is unable to do so by finding familiar elements within the word that provides clues to pronunciation.

Structural analysis means that a child can recognize the root words in words with -*s*, -*ing*, and -*ed* endings. For instance, *look* is the root word in the word *looked*. They should know what compound words are (i.e., *fire* + *man* = *fireman*). They should be able to identify common suffixes, prefixes, special word endings like -*tion*, and parts of a word or syllables.

Do this: Make a series of flash cards following this format:

Common word endings (*-s*, *-ed*, and *-ing*, as in *looks, looked, looking*)
Suffixes (*-able* as in *breakable* or *-ful* as in *hopeful*)
Prefixes (*auto-* as in *automobile* or *ex-* as in *exhale*)
Common root words
Compound words (*fireman, schoolyard, homework*, etc.)

Also try to teach the child to clap out each syllable in a difficult word. Practice this procedure using a word like *pencil*. Have them decode the word: say the word slowly, enunciating the parts. Have them clap every part: one clap for *pen* and one clap for *cil*. Ask the student how many parts they clapped. Identify each part. Say the word while clapping.

Sometimes a child attempts to pronounce a word but produces a nonsense word, mispronounces a word, or refuses to try. Help the child sound out words by looking at the letters, thinking about the sounds that those letters make, and then trying to combine the sounds. Do this first, then let the child repeat.

Also try to use repeated readings of the same word until mastery is achieved. You can also encourage children to look at the pictures to gain understanding and identification as well as context clues. (Context clues are the ideas, statements, and concepts written before and after the word that might lead to comprehension of the word within a passage.)

Sometimes, when all else fails, just tell the child the word.

Demonstrates a Lack of Confidence When Reading

Children who have difficulty with reading often experience inadequacies, feelings of inferiority, and a lack of confidence.

Do this: Use somewhat easier material for instant success. Increase difficulty later on. Reward and praise often. Apply the components of Pinpoint Reading.

Difficulty in Recognizing Words in Context

A child might be unable to get the meaning of a word, or fail to pronounce a word correctly, from the way it is embedded in a sentence. One of the best strategies to help the child arrive at the meaning or pronunciation of unknown words or phrases is through the use of context clues. Many times, children will skip words they do not know as they read silently, so you should listen to the child read orally from time to time.

Do this: Try to teach the child to identify words in context by showing examples. This strategy for decoding words and understanding their meaning is done when the reader uses the meaning of the surrounding sentences or words as a clue to understanding the unknown word or phrase.

Let's say that the troublesome word is "agreed." Place the word in a sentence and discuss it with the child.

- Example: Because all four of us decided to have pizza, we easily *agreed* on the best restaurant for having lunch together.

Sometimes provide the child with a series of sentences where only a part of a word is missing.

- Example: The _____ren were told they were being served pizza in school that day.

Students must be able to gain expertise in word recognition or word attack by reading every day, rereading their favorite stories, and using skills that involve contextual analysis or making sense of the printed word and the use of their phonics knowledge. Have them find chunks in words to pronounce, and look for clues before and after the difficult word in order to unlock its meaning.

Guesses at Words

Without using the skills already taught, students guess at words by reading the first letter or syllable and then producing an irrelevant word that comes to mind. They guess without thinking about the context of the material. They just want to get the word right as quickly as possible.

Do this: Encourage students to pay more attention to the meaning of the passage and think about what word would make the most sense. Repeat the incorrect word within the sentence and ask if it makes sense. Ask for possible words that would fit given the initial sounds of the difficult word.

For instance, when a child exhibited difficulty reading the word *fascinating* in the title of a book called *Fascinating Animals*, all one had to do was say *fas-* and they put *cin-a-ting* together after showing them the picture of elephants and explained that the word meant wonderful, amazing, colorful, and so on.

Adequate Word Attack and Word Recognition, but Poor Comprehension

A child with comprehension problems cannot understand the meaning of what was read and responds poorly to questions concerning the reading material, nor can they coherently and competently recall or retell what was just read.

Comprehension involves reading and understanding of text. If a child has problems decoding, has a small vocabulary, or reads slowly word by word, comprehension will suffer. Many times a child struggling with words, reading slowly down a page and concentrating on the details of word recognition, forgets the meaning and by the end of the passage cannot recall very many details. A multitude of comprehension skills need to be taught and addressed. Standardized test scores will probably indicate whether the student comprehends above, at, or below his grade level. Additional tests given either by the classroom teacher or by the reading specialist can further determine the problem and pinpoint specific problems with reading comprehension skills.

Do this: See the Toolbox (chapter 24) to determine which reading comprehension subskill needs to be addressed.

Inability to Skim or Scan for Information

A child might have trouble rapidly finding certain facts, phrases, critical vocabulary, or concepts asked for on tests. On standardized tests, quick retrieval of information is essential because the tests are timed.

Do this: Have children skim and scan important events in a newspaper article. Have them skim and scan for specific words or phrases in a passage. They can skim and scan for nouns, adjectives, special words or word endings, or unusual concepts and facts, and make lists of what they collected.

IDEA BANK

Here are some other ideas to try:

- Go on a scavenger hunt by looking up certain names in telephone books or events in history books.
- Play a scavenger hunt game using the dictionary. Give students a limited amount of time to find certain words.
- Play the Fast Fact Scan Game: Skim to find facts in a story with an imposed time limit. Skim to find the title, topic, topic sentence, main idea, details, main characters, solution, problems, events, actions, and other elements in the story. Teach students to be word detectives: have them locate all kinds of information and record it in a log similar to the type detectives keep when they are conducting an investigation. The detective log can contain three columns headed "Key Word Searched," "Page Number," and "Sentence Where Found."

Chapter Twenty-Four

Toolbox: The Top Twelve Skills

Children should understand that interpreting various kinds of reading passages on tests requires different kinds of strategies. They should be able to identify those tasks and set a purpose for reading. They must discriminate between reading to study for a test and reading for pleasure, and they must be able to match appropriate strategies to the reading objectives and skills called for on standardized reading/writing tests.

On the following pages, you will find comprehension skill strategies to assist children in reviewing the top twelve comprehension skills normally found on standardized literacy tests. Each skill is defined with assorted test-taking tips, sample focal question(s) normally found on exams, key test vocabulary "buzz" words signaling what kinds of information to be on the lookout for, coordinated graphic organizers to use as study aids in conjunction with that skill, and a sample task card box containing a related activity to help reinforce the skill.

CRITICAL SKILL 1: LOCATING THE MAIN IDEA

Definition: The most important idea in a paragraph is called the main idea. The main idea tells what a paragraph is mostly about. The main idea is often found in the first or last sentence of a paragraph. However, sometimes it is not found in any one sentence.

Focal Question: "What is the most important idea in this story or paragraph?"

Test-Taking Tip: The title of a reading passage usually tells something about the main idea.

Buzz Words: Be on the lookout for test questions that contain the phrases "mostly about" or "mainly about" or that ask for the "best title."

Graphic Organizer: Use the T-Chart in Appendix A to help you organize your thoughts.

Toolbox Task Card: Select a few newspaper articles from your daily paper. Cut off their headlines. Mix them up, then spread the articles on a table and read them without the headlines. After that is done, try to re-match the headlines to the appropriate article.

CRITICAL SKILL 2: FINDING FACTS AND RECALLING DETAILS

Definition: Facts and details explain or support the most important idea in the paragraph. They tell about the *who, what, where, when, why,* and *how* of the main idea. In some passages, the main idea is not exactly stated in a sentence: it is implied. In order to figure out the main idea in such a paragraph, you must think about how all the details go together. The one idea that sums up what all the details are about is the main idea. For instance, a passage could state the following: "I smile when I am happy. I frown when I am sad."

The main idea is that our faces can show our feelings. It is also important to differentiate between the topic of the story (what the whole story is about), the main idea reflected in a paragraph or series of paragraphs in the story, and details that tell more about and support the main idea.

Focal Question: "Which of these statements provides more information about the main idea of the paragraph?"

Test-Taking Tip: Since authors use facts and details in their stories, look for sentences as you read paragraph by paragraph that describe a person, place, or thing; explain how something is done; tell the order in which things or events happen; or share an experience, idea, opinion, or problem. Then look for the one sentence that best represents what the other sentences are telling you. That sentence contains the main idea and the other sentences represent the details that support the main idea.

Buzz Words: Be on the lookout for questions that contain the words *details* or *facts,* or that answer *who, what, where, when, why,* or *how.*

Graphic Organizer: Use the T-chart in Appendix A. It can help you distinguish between the main idea and the details that support it.

Toolbox Task Card: Take those headlines that you cut out in task 1. Paste a headline on top of a lined piece of paper. Make a list of all of the possible details that may have happened in the story or create your own version of the story. Write the facts and details in a logical sequence as you reconstruct the article without referring to the original one.

CRITICAL SKILL 3: SEQUENCE OF EVENTS

Definition: The order in which things happen in a story is called sequence of events. Sequence tells what happened in the beginning, middle, and end of a story or what happened first, second, third, and so on.

Focal Question: Usually test questions referring to sequence will ask the order of when things happen in a story. Questions may direct a student to place events in order from first to last.

Test-Taking Tip: Usually sequence-of-events questions involve passages that offer advice or directions on how to build something, a cooking recipe, a historical passage outlining the causes of some critical event, or biographies that detail a timeline of a person's life. Look at the title first to determine the direction of the passage.

Buzz Words: Look for words that signal sequence such as *first*, *next*, *last*, and *finally*. These words often tell what the order is in which things occur.

Graphic Organizer: Use the sequence-of-events chart in Appendix A to help you organize and recall the events as they occur in a story.

CRITICAL SKILL 4: RECOGNIZING CAUSE AND EFFECT

Definition: Many readers find it difficult to understand the logical relationships among different segments of textual material. Children should learn to focus on the causal relationships between events that happen or characters that make things happen. The cause tells the reason something happens and an effect tells what happened.

Focal Question: A cause-and-effect test question might ask the student to determine what happened and why something happened.

Test-Taking Tip: A cause may be one or many reasons why something has happened. There may be more than one cause. An effect is what happens because of the cause. There may be more than one effect. As a student reads, he or she should think about why something happens (the cause) and what happens because of the cause (the effect).

Also think about an experience or something you have previously read that might lead you to understand how one thing might cause another thing to happen.

Buzz Words: There are clue words that will warn you about a paragraph containing cause-and-effect statements. Look for these signal words: *so, as a result, if, then, because, why, therefore.*

Graphic Organizer: Use the cause-and-effect map in Appendix A to help you classify the statements and information in a reading passage.

Toolbox Task Card: Students create an "if-then" chart listing at least ten different situations such as:

If it is cloudy, then it will _____.
If you have no money, then you cannot buy _____.

CRITICAL SKILL 5: AUTHOR'S PURPOSE

Definition: Authors have a reason for writing what they did. Some may want to entertain, inform, or persuade the reader to form an opinion. A strategic and efficient reader should learn to relatively quickly pick up on the purpose of the writing and identify any subtleties and nuances of the author's reason for writing the piece. Readers who recognize an author's purpose will be better able to select reading materials suitable to match their individual needs.

Focal Question: Look for questions that ask the student to determine what the author's purpose was in the beginning or end of a passage or for basic questions that ask, "The author wrote this story mainly to _____."

Test-Taking Tip: Many test questions concerning the author's purpose are really asking the student to identify what the main idea of a passage is, why the author chose to write about that topic, and what type of audience he or she was writing for.

Buzz Words: Look for phrases such as "the author's main point" or the word "mainly."

Graphic Organizer: A chart for determining the author's purpose is given in textbox 24.1.

TEXTBOX 24.1 AUTHOR'S PURPOSE

List the statements or details in the book that fit into the three categories below. These will help you determine the author's overall purpose in writing this book.

Title of Book
Author

Entertain:
1.
2.

Persuade:
1.
2.

Persuade:
1.
2.

Toolbox Task Card: Students pretend they are authors of travel brochures who must develop a persuasive and attractive pamphlet that will entice the reader to want to travel to a foreign country. The brochure should discuss things like the country's climate, activities, attractions, lodgings, food, entertainment, and so on.

CRITICAL SKILL 6: DISTINGUISHING
BETWEEN FACT AND OPINION

Students must know that the mere fact that something is stated in a newspaper or magazine or book does not necessarily make that statement true. Students should be able to recognize those types of statements that are facts (information that is scientifically correct or observably valid) and those that are expressions of feelings, opinions, or judgments expressed by authors, and they should be able to differentiate between the two.

Children should remember that a fact is a statement that can be proven or observed; in contrast, opinions cannot be proven and often vary from person to person. Opinions may change, but facts (unless proven false), do not. In areas involving faith systems or organized religion concepts and beliefs, these parameters may not be valid. (Go try to convince our youngsters that Santa Claus does not exist or is not real!)

Focal Question: Questions usually focus on selecting a statement that cannot be supported as a fact while the other choices are indeed facts. A sample question might read, "According to this article, after concluding their research, the scientists believed which of the following statements could not be true: . . ."

Test-Taking Tip: Usually we find these types of questions involving informational content area passages in science or social studies. When in doubt about whether something is a fact or opinion, see if the statement could be true based on prior knowledge of the topic, and separate out the items that cannot possibly be proven.

Buzz Words: Sometimes in passages we find words that signal an opinion. Usually adjectives that deal with judging or evaluating, like *pretty*, *friendly*, or *beautiful*, or expressions like "I feel," "I hate," "I think," "I love," "It seems to me," and so on, are clues that an opinion is being stated.

Graphic Organizer: To help a student sift through material to distinguish facts from opinions, use the chart in figure 24.1.

Toolbox Task Card: Play a game by developing pairs of statements such as the ones listed below, and try to identify which statement in each pair is a fact and which one is an opinion.

A. Gardner Elementary School is located in Philadelphia, Pennsylvania.
B. Gardner Elementary School is the best school in the United States.

Topic: Author:

A fact is information. It is usually always true.

List the facts as you find   *List statements that prove*

Facts	Prove It
1.	1.
2.	2.
3.	3.
4.	4.
5.	5.

An opinion is what someone thinks or feels. It may or

may not be true.

List the opinions as you find   *Clue words that signal an*
them: *opinion:*

1.	1.
2.	2.
3.	3.
4.	4.
5.	5.

Figure 24.1.   Fact and Opinion Chart

Also, you could have students write about their favorite room in their house. They should tell about what actually is contained in the room and how they feel about the room. Have them list the facts and the opinions about the room they selected.

CRITICAL SKILL 7:
INTERPRETING FIGURATIVE LANGUAGE

Definition: Figurative language is the unusual and unique use of words to convey ordinary thoughts and ideas. It makes our language come alive as it helps bring out our feelings and imagination. It paints vivid pictures of people, places, and things and enhances our language and our understanding of concepts.

Similes, metaphors, and idiomatic expressions are examples of figurative language usually found in narrative stories and poetry. Children can be taught to interpret figurative language through intensive probing and discussion of reading material. Children should learn to differentiate between figurative expressions and their literal meanings. Here are some of the main types of figurative expressions:

Idiomatic Expressions: An *idiomatic expression* tells the meaning other than the literal meaning of the exact words. For example, "It rained cats and dogs today" means that it was raining heavily. Talk about the expression and its meaning, then write what you think it really means. *Idioms* are figures of speech in which the writer says one thing, but really means another. Discuss idioms used in everyday speech and record them.

Similes: A simile is a figure of speech that compares two things by using the clue words *like, as,* or *as if:* "The clouds looked like marshmallows standing still in the sky." Discuss the comparison between the clouds and marshmallows. To locate a simile, look for the key clue words *like* or *as*.

Metaphors: A metaphor is a figure of speech that compares two things without using the clue words *like* or *as*. It says that one thing is or was another thing: "The clouds are marshmallows standing still in the sky."

Poetry: Poetry is a forest full of figurative language.
Use these prompts to help a student understand a poet's message:

1. Study the title of a poem to gain insight into where the poet is going with the poem.
2. Question how the poem made you feel, see, visualize, hear, taste, or touch.
3. What words did the author use to create this mood or feeling?
4. What are the comparisons in the poem? Find them.
5. What are the figures of speech, similes, and metaphors used?
6. Can you figure out the poet's message?
7. How did you arrive at the meaning behind the poem?

8. What did you have to do to gain greater insight into the poem's message?

Focal Question: Test questions involving analysis of figurative language usually focus on comparing something to something else, so a typical question might read, "In the story, the cat's whiskers are compared to _____."

Test-Taking Tip: When learning about interpreting figurative language, the student should think about the two ideas that are being compared to one another.

Buzz Words: Questions that signal figurative language interpretation usually use the phrase "is compared to."

Graphic Organizer: As you read a poem, fable, tall tale, or other story, use the Figurative Language Chart (textbox 24.2) to glean any examples of figurative language and to determine the meaning behind the language: for each expression identified, list the objects being compared, any clue words used, and the actual meaning that the author intends to express.

Toolbox Task Card: Create a special book of figurative language expressions including similes, metaphors, and idiomatic expressions as you find them in your reading. Each page should contain the figure of speech, a meaningful sentence that fully explains the expression, and a sketch of what the expression means.

TEXTBOX 24.2 FIGURATIVE LANGUAGE CHART

Things Being Compared	*Clue Words*	*Actual Meaning*
Similes:		
1.		
2.		
Metaphors:		
1.		
2.		
Idiomatic Expressions:		
1.		
2.		

CRITICAL SKILL 8: COMPARING AND CONTRASTING

Definition: Finding how two or more things are alike and how they are different is called comparing and contrasting. Comparing involves finding out how people, places, or things are alike. Contrasting is finding out how people, places, or things are different.

Focal Question: These questions ask, "How are they alike?" "How are they different?"

Test-Taking Tip: A test item that intends for you to compare and contrast something may ask you how things are alike or how they are different.

Buzz Words: Look for signal words that show that things are alike such as *both, alike,* and *similar.* They show that things are being compared to one another. Look for signal words that show things are different such as *but, however,* and *unlike.* They show that things are being contrasted.

Graphic Organizer: Use a Venn diagram to compare and contrast events, settings, characters, and so on. On one side, list the characteristics of one subject. On the other side of the diagram, list characteristics of the other subject. The middle space or small oval is used to determine and list what the two groups have in common or share: in other words, the similarities between the subjects.

The Venn diagram is very useful when comparing and contrasting the characteristics and traits of main characters in a story. It is also helpful for taking notes and writing short essays.

Toolbox Task Card: Using the Venn diagram, determine how alike and different two members of your family are (e.g., your mother and father or two of your siblings). You could also compare friends or teachers you have had. You could also compare two summer trips you have taken to determine which one was more exciting.

CRITICAL SKILL 9: MAKING PREDICTIONS

Definition: When you think about what might happen next in a story, you are making a prediction. Recognizing what you already know and are familiar with can help you attempt a good educated guess about what might happen next.

Focal Question: Sample questions will often ask you to predict how people will behave, or which of a list of things will most likely happen.

Test-Taking Tip: Look at the title to predict what might happen in the story. Find details and facts in the story that might give you clues to what can happen next. Look at any pictures that may show what is happening and that something will occur.

Buzz Words: Questions that ask for predictions use these terms: *predict, probably, most likely.*

Graphic Organizer: Use the chart "My Predictions" (see Appendix A), to help you develop ideas about what the story, characters, and setting will be like.

Toolbox Task Card: Cut out an article from a newspaper that features a famous person who is on trial for breaking the law. After ascertaining the facts, make a prediction as to whether the person will be found guilty or not guilty and state your reasons. Then conduct a survey of your family members to determine their predictions.

CRITICAL SKILL 10: USING THE CONTEXT FOR MEANING

Definition: Let's think about what to do when a student comes across a word they cannot sound or a word or phrase that is not known or readily understood. Students should think about an alternative word that could be substituted for the mystery word so that the sentence could make sense. For example, a passage might read, "I saw a _____ run across my backyard. Phew! What a smell!" The missing word here is obviously "skunk."

Focal Question: One type of context question will probably ask, "Which phrase presents the best clue to the meaning of the word _____?"

Test-Taking Tip: One way to unlock the meaning of a word is by looking at all the information written immediately before and after the word. This is called finding the meaning of a word by using the context. The "context" is those words and phrases near the word that provide clues to the word's meaning.

Buzz Words: Look for phrases that ask a student to find the "best meaning" or "clue word."

Graphic Organizer: Use the concept word map in Appendix A to help determine the unknown word. Place the unknown word in the middle circle. In the surrounding smaller circles, add words or phrases that are found before and after the unknown word within the text. After studying the clues, try writing a sentence using the unknown word and then any associated clues to try to obtain the meaning of the unknown word.

Toolbox Task Card: Take a newspaper article and cut it into two irregularly shaped pieces. Take one section of the article and complete the puzzle by adding words or sentence fragments that would make sense.

CRITICAL SKILL 11: DRAWING CONCLUSIONS AND MAKING INFERENCES

Definition: Sometimes facts, details, or ideas are not stated directly on the page. A student might be asked to figure out (like a detective) some of the information that is missing. When you attempt to figure out something that is not directly stated in a reading passage, you are *making an inference* or *drawing a conclusion.*

Focal Question: "From the story that you have read, you can conclude that Joseph was _____."

Test-Taking Tip: Pay attention to the details in a paragraph. Use what you already know about a topic to make a viable conclusion or inference. You will be asked on a test to draw conclusions or make inferences based on action of events or on the characters' behavior.

Buzz Words: "You can conclude," "you can tell," and "you might determine" are all phrases that are used to suggest a student draw conclusions or make inferences based on the information in a passage.

Graphic Organizer: Create a chart with the headings below to help figure out information that is not stated in a reading passage:

Details in the Story, Details Not in the Story, My Conclusion

Toolbox Task Card: React to the following situation:

Two men wearing uniforms were lifting ladders and dragging hoses from the back of a huge truck.
What kind of truck was it? Explain your answer.
What were they attempting to do? Explain your answer.

CRITICAL SKILL 12: DISTINGUISHING BETWEEN FANTASY AND REALITY

Definition: People, places, or things that could exist in our world are real. Things that could not possibly happen in real life are called fantasy. Real stories are about factual events and real people, or events and people that are realistic (even if they are made up). Fantasy stories contain magic, characters possessing supernatural powers, talking animals, or imaginary places. But some stories can contain elements of both.

Focal Question: "Which of these items could not really happen?"

Test-Taking Tip: Look for stories that start with the following phrases, which indicate make-believe:

"Once upon a time . . ."
"Long ago . . ."
"In a faraway place . . ."

Buzz Words: Test questions that involve distinguishing between reality and fantasy often contain the phrases "may really happen" or "may not really happen."

Graphic Organizer: Use the Fantasy vs. Reality chart in Appendix A to separate the story elements of fantasy and reality. Fantasy stories usually are legends, myths, fables, folklore, fairy tales, tall tales, or science fiction. Real stories are usually from newspaper articles, biographies, and history.

Toolbox Task Card: Read a comic book on a famous superhero such as Superman. Locate and list those items that can be classified as real and those that are make-believe.

It's never too late to reinforce these skills regardless of whether your child exhibits a deficit in one or any of them. These critical thinking skills that your child develops now will help him/her face the challenges of college and beyond.

Therefore it is reasonable to want to maintain and strengthen your child's comprehension and study throughout their academic careers.

Some of the ways they can do this is by:

- Having your child know how to use a calendar, note pad, or some type of electronic organizer to write down assignments and plan when to accomplish the necessary work during a specific, dedicated daily time frame.
- Encourage and give support to your child to start daily homework assignments on a routinely efficient schedule. Give praise and encourage that they try to do their best on their own, then seek assistance later, if necessary.
- Do not forget to set aside a quiet area for homework and study.
- Check to make sure that all the work was done before they put everything away in their backpack.
- Good healthy food, appropriate rest, physical activity, and fun activities should always be included.
- Govern the amount of electronic time involving on-line games, vides programs, TV, cell phones, etc.
- Encouraging good school attendance is critical and always make sure that they can retrieve the day's lessons and homework that they have missed.

IDEA BANK

For this and other more exciting, creative, and worthwhile activities to strengthen your child's study skills, visit the website www.rowman.com, and type in the letters "HM" in the search box where you will find the HM Study Skills series which includes helpful study guide resources for both teachers and parents.

Chapter Twenty-Five

Useful Websites

The following is a list of websites that can assist both parents and teachers in helping children further their literacy:

- http://engageny.org/parent-guides-to-the-common-core-standards

This website offers a series of materials, guides, and links geared to help parents and teachers understand the Common Core Standards. This site is sponsored by the New York City and New York State Departments of Education, but is relevant to parents in all states.

- http://www.teachersfirst.com/professional-resources/working-with -parents.cfm

TeachersFirst is a website that offers practical advice and ideas on how teachers can best work together effectively and cooperatively with parents.

- http://www.teachersandfamilies.com/open/tr/tr3.cfm

This site offers outstanding practical suggestions and tips designed to help children become better strategic readers.

- http://www.readwritethink.org/about/standards.html

This website allows teachers to browse language arts lesson plans and enables teachers to select a standards tab to see how the lesson aligns with their state's particular set of standards.

Chapter Twenty-Six

Final Thoughts

Walt Disney once said: "There is more treasure in books than in all the pirate's loot on Treasure Island." The current thinking about test preparation and the teaching of reading and language arts is that children, in order to succeed in school and in their careers, must start to read many different types or genres of books. An abundance of fiction and non-fiction works which can include, but are not limited to, classical works and contemporary books should be read.

Yet, the most important book is the one they want to read and not have to read because the teacher said so or the test mandates it. The most important life skills indeed include reading for meaning or comprehension, interpreting what they read, judging and evaluating texts, and developing a genuine liking, appreciation, and respect for the act or behavior we call reading.

It comes down to whether they prefer riding a skateboard all day or reaching a compromise between skateboarding and book reading.

It is important to remember that common core standards based assessments require children to read more deeply and to make more intensive, exhaustive interpretations and connections to the test literature. This is why it behooves teachers and parents to guide their children into greater deeper critical thought.

Critical thinking is a taught skill and is never assumed no matter what a child's intellect is. It is an acquired skill of analyzing and evaluating ideas and concepts on the go as a child reads through a passage. As your child reads through, they must be taught to self-direct and self-monitor, and even self-correct their thinking about the test materials and about literature.

Children should question everything and leave nothing behind unknown or unanswered. They should constantly be speculating and deducing as they read metacognitively with these questions in mind:

1. What am I reading this for?
2. What am I searching for?
3. What information do I need here to answer the question?
4. I need help; who do I ask?
5. I need help; I'll jot down what confuses me in my reading journal.
6. What conclusions can I reach about the characters or events in the story?
7. What is the main point, idea, or thesis of this passage?
8. What can I assume from these words and sentences?
9. Is there anything I can imply from this passage?
10. What is the author's point of view?
11. What is my point of view?

But teachers and parents have to take it deeper. We have a new responsibility to avoid trite, useless, and banal questions. Once while observing a middle school social studies teacher insist that her students determine the color of Alexander the Great's "horse," the teacher became irate because no one knew the answer. The teacher was merely reading the question from a prepared text book publishers' study guide; but that is no excuse.

Or how about the English teacher who simply and mindlessly read a novel to the class while the students just sat and passively listened, completely bored and inattentive. Amazing right?, but sad nevertheless.

Mere recall of facts in previously learned material is developing a quiz-show mentality among our students. It is necessary to some extent, but it is not the only skill. Sure we want our children to be knowledgeable about historical events and when they occurred, but our children must learn to achieve greater understanding by attempting to bring meaning to the written text.

Children must learn to problem solve and find solutions and alternatives. They must also learn to apply what they have learned in school and life's lessons to find the necessary answers to personal and societal problems and predicaments. In addition, they need to deeply analyze written material, their own and others, so that the whole and its parts can be clearly understood and to make clear what are truths from falsehoods and what concepts are real and unreal to them.

Our children must also evaluate what they know in printed matter and in written discourse so they can be better able to make decisive and incisive judgments about new concepts expressed especially in the media and on the Internet.

And they must be able to take from their past experiences and storehouses of knowledge and build new strategies, structures, new ideas, or at the very least have the opportunity at trying a new way to make things better or to try new patterns that can help them create new meaning.

My father imparted his belief that one must strive in life to "make it good." We owe it to our children to support them, raise them up to new heights, have them overcome their fears, and show them the worth and the intrinsic need and desire of a good education. Let's help them "make it good."

Appendix A:
Graphic Organizers, Templates, Forms

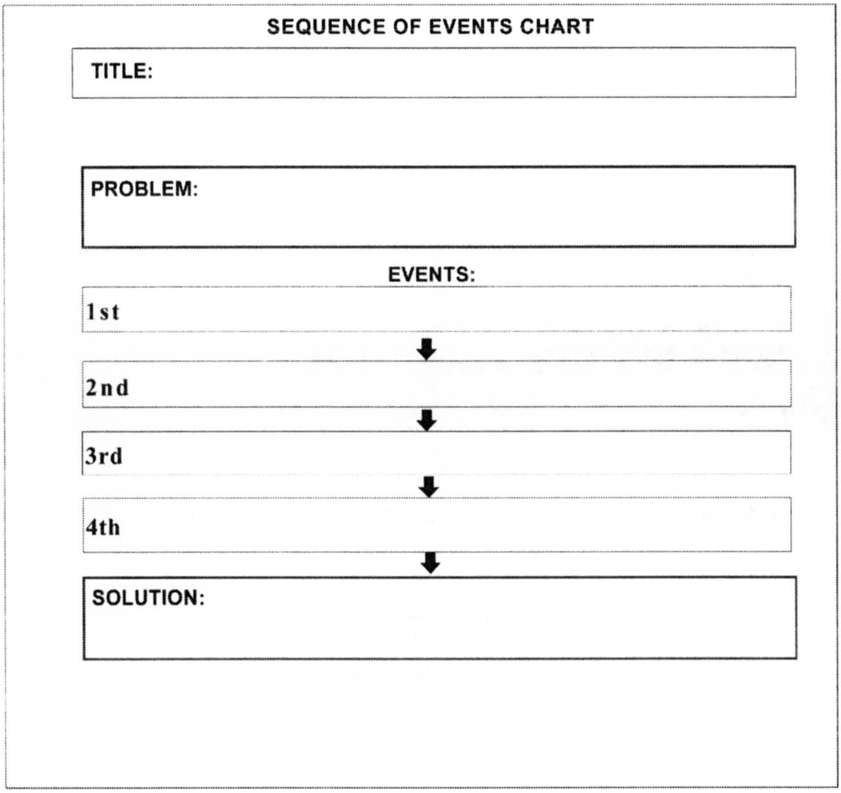

SEQUENCE OF EVENTS CHART

TITLE:

PROBLEM:

EVENTS:

1st

2nd

3rd

4th

SOLUTION:

Figure A.1.

MY PREDICTIONS

Title _____

Author _____

**I think this story will be
about** _____
_____
_____

**I think the characters will
probably** _____
_____
_____
_____

**It looks like this story takes
place** _____

I guess that the following things may happen:

_____
_____
_____

Figure A.2.

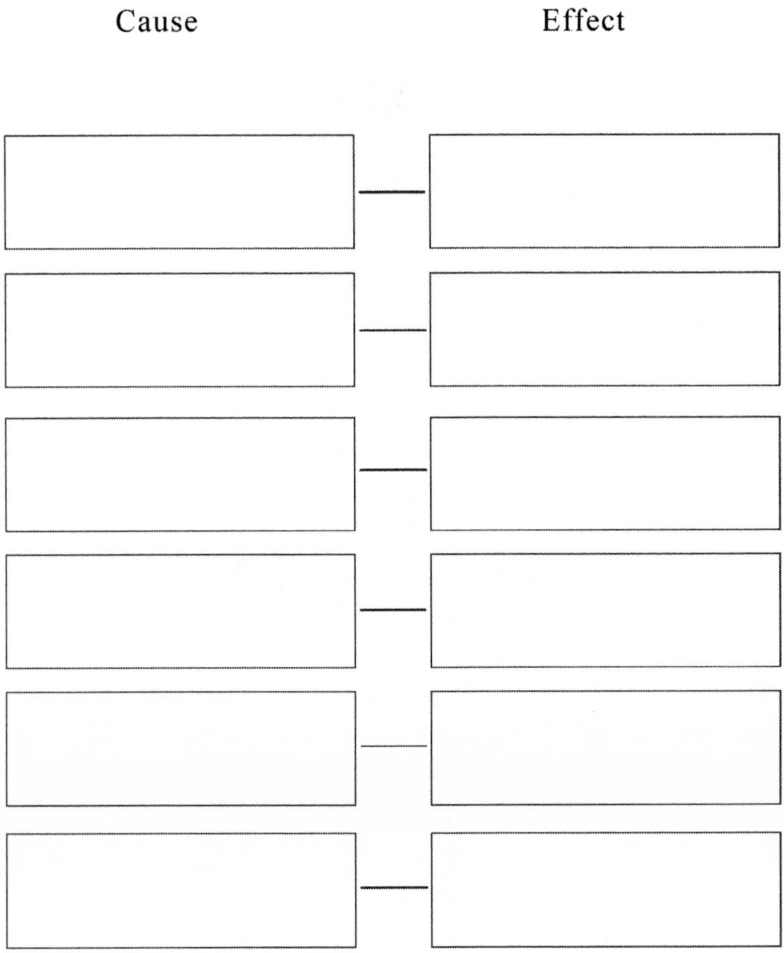

Cause   Effect

Figure A.3.   Cause and Effect Chart

FANTASY   REALITY

Story Title		Story Title
Characters		Subject
Unreal Elements		Facts

Figure A.4.   Fantasy vs. Reality Chart.

PRESS RELEASE

Date:_____

From: _____

To: (List name of newspaper)

Special Event: _____

Date of Event: _____

Time: _____

Place: _____

DESCRIPTION OF EVENT

_____

_____

_____

_____

_____

_____

_____

_____

_____

_____

_____

_____

Contact Person: (Your Name)

Telephone: _____

FINDING THE MAIN IDEA-T CHART
TOPIC-
MAIN IDEA-

MAJOR SUPPORTING DETAILS
1.
2.
3.
4.
5.

Figure A.5.

Title of Book:	
Author:	
Type: Check One ❑ Novel ❑ Biography ❑ Non-Fiction ❑ Other	
Plot: (What This Book Was About)	
Main Characters:	
Evaluation:	
I liked (didn't like) this story because	
This story was real (unreal) because	

New Vocabulary:	
Word	Dictionary Definition

Figure A.6. Mini Book Report Form

Appendix B:
Sample Story with Lesson Plan

The following story is real. It was told to me by my father concerning his life in Europe prior to World War II. What he said, I wrote down. I asked some questions. Some of which he could not remember the answers to or because circumstances were so painful that it locked his memory forever.

I feel a parent or teacher can use this story and accompanying lesson plan as part of the activities within this book as well as to encourage deeper thinking about life and about how history can radically change people's lives.

The activities for this read-aloud story are broken down into before, during, and after the reading.

BEFORE

It is important to share with children the historical underpinnings of this story which occurred prior to World War II. Preliminary discussions should center on the rein of Nazi dictator Adolf Hitler, his rise to power, and his belligerence and treatment of Jewish people in Europe before the outbreak of the war. It may be helpful to visit the website of the United States Holocaust Museum in Washington, D.C., and other relevant sites dealing with this issue. The term "Anschluss" is particularly critical because it led to the annexing of Austria, due to the nefarious and coercive actions of Germany, where my father worked and lived. Phony and contrived elections were held in Austria and as a result, the country approved of the German takeover. Since my father was Jewish, he felt threatened and subsequently felt his life in peril by this plot. If there were no war, he would have remained in Austria, would have no need to emigrate to the United States, and among other things, I would not have been born.

Throughout the story, children can attempt to make relevant connections between my father's poor life in Poland, where he lived and grew up, and his experiences in Austria. They can write their connections to their own lives as well as to other texts they may have read in the past. They can also make connections to the community and with the world around them. It is important they journal their feelings making text-to-self, text-to-other text, and text to community/world as they listen to this story. Children should be able to search for deeper understandings of the story when they attempt to connect to the story at their own level of consciousness.

One way to record feelings is through the use of a story reaction journal entry where on one side of the page children write what they listened to and on the other side of the paper they can write their personal reactions and responses as well as inquiries.

DURING

During the reading, children can stop and analyze what has occurred through the emphasis of critical sections of this memoir. Children can learn to make personal ties to my father's story by focusing on text-to-self connections such as:

1. What so far does this story remind you of?
2. Can you share your feelings about my father?
3. Can you relate anything in your life, past or present, that you can connect with my father's life?

You can also ask questions as to whether they can relate this story to other stories that they may have read at home or in school such as:

1. Does my father's story remind you of another story or book you have read?

2. Does this story have the same parts and structure to other things you have read?
3. Is this story different from other stories you have read. Explain.

And lastly, they can make text-to-community or world connections by asking:

1. Does this story remind you of similar events that have happened in the world?
2. Are the events and circumstances similar or different to what you have read about real events in world history?
3. Talk and share, then have children write in their journals. Think of possibly modeling a sample response of what the nature of a journal entry might look like. Discuss their entries by having them read excerpts aloud for input and clarification by the rest of the class.

AFTER

Instead of the mundane test or quiz, encourage children to develop some form of final exit project where they can work either individually, in partnerships, or small groups. Sample projects may include:

1. A vocabulary/dictionary of Jewish/Yiddish words that have been mentioned in the text.
2. Students can write a paper on prejudice, racism, bias, and anti-semitism and how solutions to these societal problems can be achieved.
3. They can pretend that they are reporters writing about the problems Jews faced prior to and during World War II.
4. They can create a mock interview session interviewing my dad as he lived as a boy in Poland, as a young entrepreneur in Vienna, Austria, and on his escape to freedom to America.
5. They could develop story extenders whereby they can add to what they think may have happened to my father after he landed safely in America.
6. Ask children to develop annotated bibliographies of similar genre books and present them to the class.

7. Ask children to role play my father and other characters in the story.
8. Interpret and analyze the only picture I have of my father posing with other co-workers in front of his tailor shop in downtown Vienna. When I went to look for the shop in 1972, it was gone only to be replaced by a modern housing complex. But the name of the street still existed as did a carousel up the block.
9. Children may want to record some questions they would like to ask of me and how I felt listening to my father reminisce and how I got him to reluctantly and painfully say what he did. If you were my father, what would you have done? How would you have escaped? Ask children to conceive of a new escape plan or new circumstances. Or, would you have wanted to escape at all?
10. Children can draw sketches of the events in chronological order that led up to my father's hasty departure from Vienna.
11. Children can research and write a tourist snapshot on the rich history of Vienna including the historical sites, famous people from Austria, the foods, maps, flag, geographical features, language, etc.
12. Ask children to write a review as they recommend this story to other children. Have them explain why they liked or disliked the story.
13. And lastly, since my father safely traveled to freedom on a luxury ship called the *Queen Mary*, children can research the history of this boat, the significance of its name, etc., and how they can relate their own experiences on cruising trips with their parents.

FOLLOW-UP

Children present their projects in class and at home and discuss what they did, how they did it, the problems or obstacles they faced, and what they learned. In classrooms, the other students can take notes and have an opportunity to ask questions, make appropriate comments, and give praise. At home, parents can invite family, friends, and neighbors to attend this presentation. The main thing is to just simply share in what happened to my father and why.

THE COAT MY FATHER WORE

This is my father, Ben Schneider. He was a tailor, like his father was and possibly just like his father's father and maybe even further back than that. That's how we got our family name. In German, "Schneider" means cutter or tailor.

His family lived in Poland, in a small town, or as they called them "shetels." The land was flat with some forests and lakes. The streets were unpaved. The roads were made of dirt so when it rained, everything turned a muddy brown. When the hot summer winds blew, the dust kicked up everywhere. It was a crowded town and people were packed into little houses. Since the town was near a river, water carriers took barrels hoisted on their shoulders, one on each side, drew their water, and brought them into town. You traveled mostly by foot. The town itself maybe had only a few hundred people.

My father had two brothers and two sisters. His mother and father were poor and plain, God-fearing, pious, and respectable. They had only two loves: God and family. The only joy their family could possibly have was not from becoming rich, but to have joy from its children. Every parent dreamed of having a son become a scholar and every daughter the wife of one. This was how you were rich. But besides this and even more importantly than food or water, like everything else in the shetel, one needed a certain modicum of "mazel" or luck to get by. He said, "We needed mazel in those days to be healthy, to grow up healthy, and to have a good life."

As a young boy, he watched his father sew. The needle punctured the cloth and came out the other side as the spool of thread got smaller and smaller. And this happened again, and again, and again. All day long, his mother cooked and cleaned, milked the cow, and kindled the fire for her oven. His father was religious and studied as a daily routine. His mother made sure they were fed properly and was overly cautious about their health and safety. Ben had to be good to his parents and study hard in school.

The townspeople were very well behaved so they did not need policemen. But they did have a fire department. There was one doctor but no hospital. Once when he was a small boy, he developed a mysterious illness with a high fever. No one knew what it was. He got very sick. His parents summoned the doctor and he was given some kind of medicine. After a few days, the fever broke. "It was close, Benny could have died," the doctor said. Many young people died of things they did not know about. "I never knew what sickness I had," he said. "I guess I was just lucky."

They lived in a ramshackle two room hut made of logs. It was cold in the winter and hot in summertime. His feet touched a dirt and straw floor. It felt hard, damp, and cold. Planks of wood framed holes in the wall for makeshift windows without glass. Straw and some wood made the roof leak when it rained. It was crowded and without privacy. Everyone slept together and ate meals together. Airless and sunless, it smelled most of the time from the odors of people and animals. This was his best home, his only home. He thought: "This was the best place to live."

Ben had a garden where he grew potatoes and where he kept his chickens and geese. He had a pet goose he raised from birth. Every day he would feed it and play with it. In no time, the goose grew large and soon it would no longer serve as his pet. Another favorite of his was a lamb. He fed it and made sure it was healthy. He would stroke its fur and kiss it. But then it got too old, and the day of reckoning had begun. His father told him to take it to the town "shohet." His job was to ritually slaughter animals for food and for a fee would kill what needed killing. Although not liking this idea, my father realized what had to be done. Without animals, there would be no meal. As a young boy he and his friends used to peek through the slats of the slaughterer's hut to see how it happened. He listened for the soft prayers coming from within then saw the knife. That night he ate chicken, gefilte fish, and chicken soup. But eating the meat from his pet was something else as he said: "I couldn't do it."

Then there was bath night. "We took family baths twice a year," he said as I looked at him with a funny uncomprehending stare. His parents went first, one at a time, into the barrel which served as a tub. Then his brothers and sisters using the same water, mind you, and took their turn. When it was his turn, the water, by then, turned a milky gray with floating stuff in it. Afterward, the neighbors came and bathed as well. "You could imagine that everyone smelled most of the time," he said, "and we also had lice which made us scratch and itch. But otherwise, we were a clean family."

He had fun. He played soccer and watched his sisters play with dolls made from potatoes or apples. Music was played during a festival called Purim while they ate triangular cookies called "humentashen." During another holiday known as Hanukkah, he played with dreidels which were toplike spinning toys made of wood. But when the Sabbath came, or Shabbos as it was called, on a Friday night and lasted till Saturday night, you were not allowed to do anything except eat, sleep, go for a walk, and pray in the synagogue. Shabbos was a special and very holy day of the week.

When market day came, all the farmers would gather from the surrounding countryside and set up their wares in the center of the town square by the water well. You could buy chickens, geese, ducks, calves, goats, vegetables, fruits, shoes, candy, groceries, and hardware. The merchants who owned shops around the square would sweep their floors, print signs, arrange their goods, check their scales, and display their own foods, fabrics, bread, cakes, cookies , candy, and new and used clothing. It was during market day that my father met people that his parents would refer to as "goyim." My father wasn't sure who they were, only he felt that "they weren't our people," he said.

He knew that "they were strangers to us because they did not live with us and because they were not Jewish," he said. Then he explained: "You see Stevie, living in Poland made us think of ourselves as Jews first, Polish second." The entire town was mainly Jewish and my father had only Jewish friends. The Jews lived amongst themselves and these outsiders were shunned. But who shunned whom? "We distrusted them, we were uncomfortable and we feared them," he said. So my father told me not to talk to them nor play with their kids. He kept saying: "They didn't like us and we didn't like them, you understand." It was the religion, our religion that separated us and made us feel that we were different from them and they from us. I just shook my head in agreement. But the one thing they did have in common, according to my father, was that "everyone was poor."

The fount of our religion and religious events centered on what the people called "Schul," or the synagogue. The schul was the tallest building in the shtetl. It was here that the study of the Jewish religion took place. This was the place where the townspeople prayed to God. This was where the people were taught how to pray and how to serve God and to hope for the coming of the Messiah when the entire world would know everlasting peace. Their lives were dedicated to inner discipline and self-control. Each individual was responsible to God. There was much time given to prayer, rituals, and fasting. People loved to study. "Our leader, the Rabbi, our teacher, would always be seen studying, writing, and counseling members of our community. This was where I went to begin to learn how to be a good Jewish person," he said.

This is how my father told me how he learned to be a good Jew:

"When I was a small boy, my parents wrapped me in a prayer shawl called a 'tallis' and hustled me off to the 'cheder' or Hebrew school. The school was located in a small room inside the synagogue. There were large wooden tables with long benches. My teacher, whom we called a 'melamed' shoved a tablet with Hebrew letters in my face and we sat and listened as he taught us how to read the Hebrew alphabet so that we could someday read in Hebrew. We also learned 'Torah' or the five holy books of Moses which was the law that God gave to Moses. I also learned to read from a Sidd ur or prayer book. We were also taught about customs, traditions, and the Holy Land known as Israel. If we were caught napping or fooling around, he would hit us with a wooden stick. Most of all I remember being taught to be God-fearing, to do kind acts and deeds called 'mitzvoth,' and to strive to be educated, charitable, and responsible to my parents and the community. I turned out to be a good Jew but not very pious. I didn't think God would punish me because I didn't feel that religious. I always thought that it was more important to feel Jewish rather than to always study about it," he said.

When his thirteenth birthday came, he was a Bar Mitzvah. This special day would transform him into becoming a man. From then on all his good deeds and sins would no longer be charged to the account of his father. After the ceremony in schul, he had a party to celebrate this transitional moment in his life. "I was given a few pieces of candy, cake, and had some wine. Some party!"

His mother sewed. His father sewed. Ben watched them carefully and learned the Schneider trade. A trade that spanned generations in his family. "I learned from them and decided to tailor," he said. "We made some of our own clothes, but mostly we worked at repairing other people's clothes. After all, what was I supposed to do with my life anyway. If you didn't know anything else, you became what your father was and I didn't know anything else," he said.

But my dad became restless in the shetel. Sewing all day made him that way. There were very few opportunities for young men his age. Then a letter came. It said that he was to be drafted into the Polish army. This was no good. It meant a life of hard labor, punishment, or worse especially for a young Jewish boy. "I had to decide right then and there whether to go into the army or leave my family and escape. I had no choice," he said.

Ben Schneider decided to leave as other Jewish boys did. He left home rather than join the Polish army in search for hope and prosperity. His travels took him to Vienna, the capital of Austria. Vienna was sophisticated, cosmopolitan, cultured, and huge compared with the small town from whence he came. "I really didn't want to leave. But I had to," he said. "I prayed to God to give me strength and a little bit of mazel," he said.

He managed to set up a tailoring shop at 10 Praterstrasse in Vienna. He had his own label, which was sewn into every piece of clothing his store produced. He made clothes mainly for women. He started to make money, friends, bought his own apartment, had money in the bank, and even spent his summers with his friends vacationing in Yugoslavia on the beaches of the Adriatic or took to the mountains of Austria to luxuriate in its serenity, beauty, and peacefulness. In winter, to protect himself from Vienna's biting chill, he made himself a black overcoat with a warm lining. He used to make these same coats for me and for my mother and sister. These were golden times for he was now referred to as "Herr" Schneider. He seemed to have gotten at least some mazel. The shetel was beginning to become a faded memory but his family never left his heart.

Then a man named Adolf Hitler came to power in Germany, a country next door to Austria. As his rise to power became unabated, Hitler spread a powerful message of personal hatred against Jewish people living not only in Europe, but throughout the world. My father began to feel uneasy especially over the way people now talked and looked at him. This vicious kind of anti-semitism spread throughout Austria. Life was changing rapidly. Hitler's sphere of influence soon engulfed all of Austria as Germany sought to annex and make it a part of what the German leader called his "Third Reich." Mazel seemed to vanish overnight. "There was going to be trouble for the Jews," he said. "I began to feel afraid."

His business started to suffer. No one came to his shop anymore when they found out that he was Jewish. One morning he came to work only to find racial epithets scrawled in paint across the front window. One night a rock was thrown into that same window and broken shards of glass was strewn over the sidewalk glistening in the shadows cast by the streetlamps. The rock was strapped with the ubiquitous message, "Dirty Jew." He was unable to concentrate on his sewing. Fearing persecution and increasing hardship, he reluctantly made a decision to leave his home, business, and friends. In short time, his worst fears were realized. "It was not safe to live as a Jewish person in Vienna," he said. "I kept thinking about the village slaughterer, the shohet intoning prayers as he killed the livestock. Was I the next lamb?"

The Austrian government became a Nazi puppet regime and the police were of no help. Then, one night, an obtrusive knock on the front door of his home brought the secret police. He was arrested and taken to jail. Since he registered to become an American citizen with the U.S. Embassy, a lawyer was able to obtain his release. As he sat in jail with other innocent Jews, he wondered what he had done wrong. Would he be killed? He wondered why someone like Hitler and his Austrian Nazi sympathizers hated Jews so much. "We were a simple people who only wanted to live in peace, and to work, and to be free," he said.

It was growing too dangerous. People were being arrested daily and some sent away to concentration camps. His decision made, he quickly packed a small valise with only a few clothes. He opened a strongbox he kept hidden in a closet, removed all of its contents, closed his bank accounts, and purchased a one-way ticket on a ship bound to take him to freedom in America.

He took his heavy black overcoat and with his best tool of his trade, the scissors, deftly cut a swath in the bottom inner lining. He stuffed the slit with all the money he saved. Then he sewed it back up again. The black thread held the seam tightly; the money, safe.

He set sail for America the next day on an ocean liner called the *Queen Mary*. Before boarding, two Nazi policemen dressed in brown uniforms and wearing armbands showing a black twisted cross in a red circle looked at his identity papers and passport. They absconded with his wallet which had a few tempting dollars used as bait money, his watch, and a gold ring ripped from his pinky finger. His remaining wealth was tucked away inside his coat lining which they never bothered to inspect.

As he came on board and took a stroll on the deck, he patted the bottom-lining and softly smiled knowing that he would land in America not totally poor.

As the ship set sail that afternoon, he could see the coastline of Europe slowly melt into the gray mist of a cold, damp March day. As he stood along the upper deck railing, he took one last, long look and said good-bye to his family. A family he would never forget. A family he might never see or hear from again.

My father lived to be ninety-three. He used the money he hid to help him start a new life in America. He worked, of course, as a tailor in New York City. He married. Had me and my sister and eventually had many grandchildren. He applied and received a pension from the Austrian government as reparations for his business and bank assets that were plundered by the Nazi Austrian government. The coat, by now moth eaten and tattered, had hung in a hall closet until it was disposed of years later, like so many painful memories his heart and mind refused to give up. Much of his family perished in the firestorm that later engulfed Europe after he fled. Only one sister and one brother made it out safely. They had mazel, and so did he.

For further reading on this topic:

Fiction: Lois Lowry—*Number the Stars*
Non-Fiction: Anne Frank—*The Diary of a Young Girl*

References

Izzo, C. V., Weissberg, R. P., Kasprow, W. J., and Fendrich, M. (1999). A longitudinal assessment of teacher perceptions of parent involvement in children's education and school performance. *American Journal of Community Psychology, 27*(6), 817–39.

Mapp, K. L. (2003). Having their say: Parents describe why and how they are engaged in their children's learning. *The School Community Journal, 13*(1), 35–64.

National Institute of Child Health and Human Development. (2000). *Report of the National Reading Panel: Teaching children to read: An evidence-based assessment of the scientific research literature on reading and its implications for reading instruction.* Retrieved June 6, 2005, from http:// www.nichd.nih .gov/publications/nrp/smallbook.htm.

Shaver, A. V., & Walls, R. T. (1998). Effect of Title I parent involvement on student reading and mathematics achievement. *Journal of Research and Development in Education, 31*(2), 90–91.

CPSIA information can be obtained at www.ICGtesting.com
Printed in the USA
BVOW07*1619131213

338971BV00002B/3/P

9 781610 489591